Contents

CHAPTER I

The Buddhist Attitude of Mind

THE FOUR NOBLE TRUTHS

CHAPTER II

The First Noble Truth: *Dukkha*

CHAPTER III

The Second Noble Truth: *Samudaya*: 'The Arising of *Dukkha*'

CHAPTER IV

The Third Noble Truth: *Nirodha*: 'The Cessation of *Dukkha*'—

Illustrations

VIII.   Head of the Buddha. Hadda, Afghanistan. Stucco. Graeco-Indian style, 3rd to 4th century A.C. Musée Guimet, Paris. *By courtesy of the Musée Guimet, Paris.*

IX.   The Buddha. Prah Khan, Cambodia. Khmer Art, Bayon style. 12th century A.C. Musée Guimet, Paris.
By courtesy of the Musée Guimet, Paris.

X.   *Saṃsāra-cakra or Bhava-cakra*, the Cycle of Existence and Continuity. Tibet. Museum für Völkerkunde, Hamburg. *By courtesy of the Musée Guimet, Paris.*

Foreword

by Paul Demiéville

Member of the Institut de France,
Professor at the Collège de France
Director of Buddhist Studies at the School
of Higher Studies (Paris)

Here is an exposition of Buddhism conceived in a resolutely modern spirit by one of the most qualified and enlightened representatives of that religion. The Rev. Dr. W. Rahula received the traditional training and education of a Buddhist monk in Ceylon, and held eminent positions in one of the leading monastic institutes (Pirivena) in that island, where the Law of the Buddha flourishes from the time of Asoka and has preserved all its vitality up to this day. Thus brought up in an ancient tradition, he decided, at this time when all traditions are called in question, to face the spirit and the methods of international scientific learning. He entered the Ceylon University, obtained the B.A. Honours degree (London), and then won the degree of Doctor of Philosophy of the Ceylon University on a highly learned thesis on the History of Buddhism in Ceylon. Having worked with distinguished professors at the University of Calcutta and come in contact with adepts of Mahāyāna (the Great Vehicle), that form of Buddhism which reigns from Tibet to the Far East, he decided to go into the Tibetan and Chinese texts in order to widen his œcumenism, and he has honoured us by coming to the University of Paris (Sorbonne) to prepare a study of Asanga, the illustrious philosopher of Mahāyāna, whose principal works in the original Sanskrit are lost, and can only be read in their Tibetan and Chinese translations. It is now eight years since Dr. Rahula is among us, wearing the yellow robe, breathing the air of the Occident, searching perhaps in our old troubled mirror a universalized reflection of the religion which is his.

The book, which he has kindly asked me to present to the public of the West, is a luminous account, within reach of everybody, of the fundamental principles of the Buddhist doctrine, as they are found in the most ancient texts, which are called 'The Tradition' (*Āgama*) in Sanskrit and 'The Canonic Corpus' (*Nikāya*) in Pali. Dr. Rahula, who possesses an incomparable knowledge of these texts, refers to them constantly and almost exclusively. Their authority is recognized unanimously by all the Buddhist schools, which were and are numerous, but none of which ever deviates from these texts, except with the intention of better interpreting the spirit beyond the letter. The interpretation has indeed been varied in the course of the expansion of Buddhism through many centuries and vast regions, and the Law has taken more than one aspect. But the aspect of Buddhism here presented by Dr. Rahula—humanist, rational, Socratic in some respects, Evangelic in others, or again almost scientific—has for its support a great deal of authentic scriptural evidence which he only had to let speak for themselves.

The explanations which he adds to his quotations, always translated with scrupulous accuracy, are clear, simple, direct, and free from all pedantry. Some among them might lead to discussion, as when he wishes to rediscover in the Pali sources all the doctrines of Mahāyāna; but his familiarity with those sources permits him to throw new light on them. He addresses himself to the modern man, but he refrains from insisting on comparisons just suggested here and there, which could be made with certain currents of thought of the contemporary world: socialism, atheism, existentialism, psycho-analysis. It is for the reader to appreciate the modernity, the possibilities of adaptation of a doctrine which, in this work of genuine scholarship, is presented to him in its primal richness.

Preface

All over the world today there is growing interest in Buddhism. Numerous societies and study-groups have come into being, and scores of books have appeared on the teaching of the Buddha. It is to be regretted, however, that most of them have been written by those who are not really competent, or who bring to their task misleading assumptions derived from other religions, which must misinterpret and misrepresent their subject. A professor of comparative religion who recently wrote a book on Buddhism did not even know that Ānanda, the devoted attendant of the Buddha, was a *bhikkhu* (a monk), but thought he was a layman! The knowledge of Buddhism propagated by books like these can be left to the reader's imagination.

I have tried in this little book to address myself first of all to the educated and intelligent general reader, uninstructed in the subject, who would like to know what the Buddha actually taught. For his benefit I have aimed at giving briefly, and as directly and simply as possible, a faithful and accurate account of the actual words used by the Buddha as they are to be found in the original Pali texts of the *Tipiṭaka*, universally accepted by scholars as the earliest extant records of the teachings of the Buddha. The material used and the passages quoted here are taken directly from these originals. In a few places I have referred to some later works too.

I have borne in mind, too, the reader who has already some knowledge of what the Buddha taught and would like to go further with his studies. I have therefore provided not only the Pali equivalents of most of the key-words, but also references to the original texts in footnotes, and a select bibliography.

The difficulties of my task have been manifold: throughout I have tried to steer a course between the unfamiliar and the popular, to give the English reader of the present day something which he could understand and appreciate, without sacrificing anything of the matter and the form of the discourses of the

Buddha. Writing the book I have had the ancient texts running in my mind, so I have deliberately kept the synonyms and repetitions which were a part of the Buddha's speech as it has come down to us through oral tradition, in order that the reader should have some notion of the form used by the Teacher. I have kept as close as I could to the originals, and have tried to make my translations easy and readable.

But there is a point beyond which it is difficult to take an idea without losing in the interests of simplicity the particular meaning the Buddha was interested in developing. As the title 'What the Buddha Taught' was selected for this book, I felt that it would be wrong not to set down the words of the Buddha, even the figures he used, in preference to a rendering which might provide the easy gratification of comprehensibility at the risk of distortion of meaning.

I have discussed in this book almost everything which is commonly accepted as the essential and fundamental teaching of the Buddha. These are the doctrines of the Four Noble Truths, the Noble Eightfold Path, the Five Aggregates, Karma, Rebirth, Conditioned Genesis (*Paṭiccasamuppāda*), the doctrine of No-Soul (*Anatta*), *Satipaṭṭhāna* (the Setting-up of Mindfulness). Naturally there will be in the discussion expressions which must be unfamiliar to the Western reader. I would ask him, if he is interested, to take up on his first reading the opening chapter, and then go on to Chapters V, VII and VIII, returning to Chapters II, III, IV and VI when the general sense is clearer and more vivid. It would not be possible to write a book on the teaching of the Buddha without dealing with the subjects which *Theravāda* and *Mahāyāna* Buddhism have accepted as fundamental in his system of thought.

The term *Theravāda—Hīnayāna* or 'Small Vehicle' is no longer used in informed circles—could be translated as 'the School of the Elders' (*theras*), and *Mahāyāna* as 'Great Vehicle'. They are used of the two main forms of Buddhism known in the world today. *Theravāda,* which is regarded as the original orthodox Buddhism, is followed in Ceylon, Burma, Thailand, Cambodia, Laos, and Chittagong in East Pakistan. *Mahāyāna*, which developed relatively later, is followed in other Buddhist countries like China, Japan, Tibet, Mongolia, etc. There are certain differences, mainly with regard to some beliefs, practices and observances between these two schools, but on the most important teachings of the Buddha, such as those discussed here, *Theravāda* and *Mahāyāna* are unanimously agreed.

It only remains for me now to express my sense of gratitude to Professor E. F. C. Ludowyk, who in fact invited me to write this book, for all the help given me, the interest taken in it, the suggestions he offered, and for reading through the manuscript. To Miss Marianne Möhn too, who went through the manuscript and made valuable suggestions, I am deeply grateful. Finally I am greatly beholden to Professor Paul Demiéville, my teacher in Paris, for his kindness in writing the Foreword.

W. Rahula

Paris
July 1958

To Mani

Sabbadānaṃ dhammadānaṃ jināti
'The gift of Truth excels all other gifts'

The Buddha

The Buddha, whose personal name was Siddhattha (Siddhārtha in Sanskrit), and family name Gotama (Skt. Gautama), lived in North India in the 6th century B.C. His father, Suddhodana, was the ruler of the kingdom of the Sākyas (in modern Nepal). His mother was queen Māyā. According to the custom of the time, he was married quite young, at the age of sixteen, to a beautiful and devoted young princess named Yasodharā. The young prince lived in his palace with every luxury at his command. But all of a sudden, confronted with the reality of life and the suffering of mankind, he decided to find the solution—the way out of this universal suffering. At the age of 29, soon after the birth of his only child, Rāhula, he left his kingdom and became an ascetic in search of this solution.

For six years the ascetic Gotama wandered about the valley of the Ganges, meeting famous religious teachers, studying and following their systems and methods, and submitting himself to rigorous ascetic practices. They did not satisfy him. So he abandoned all traditional religions and their methods and went his own way. It was thus that one evening, seated under a tree (since then known as the Bodhi- or Bo-tree, 'the Tree of Wisdom'), on the bank of the river Neranjarā at Buddha-Gaya (near Gaya in modern Bihar), at the age of 35, Gotama attained Enlightenment, after which he was known as the Buddha, 'The Enlightened One'.

After his Enlightenment, Gotama the Buddha delivered his first sermon to a group of five ascetics, his old colleagues, in the Deer Park at Isipatana (modern Sarnath) near Benares. Since that day, for 45 years, he taught all classes of men and women—kings and peasants, Brahmins and outcasts, bankers and beggars, holy men and robbers—without making the slightest distinction between them. He recognized no differences of caste or social groupings, and the Way he preached was open to all men and women who were ready to understand and to follow it.

At the age of 80, the Buddha passed away at Kusinārā (in modern Uttar Pradesh).

Today Buddhism is found in Ceylon, Burma, Thailand, Cambodia, Laos, Vietnam, Tibet, China, Japan, Mongolia, Korea, Formosa, in some parts of India, Pakistan and Nepal, and also in the Soviet Union. The Buddhist population of the world is over 500 million.

CHAPTER I

THE BUDDHIST ATTITUDE OF MIND

Among the founders of religions the Buddha (if we are permitted to call him the founder of a religion in the popular sense of the term) was the only teacher who did not claim to be other than a human being, pure and simple. Other teachers were either God, or his incarnations in different forms, or inspired by him. The Buddha was not only a human being; he claimed no inspiration from any god or external power either. He attributed all his realization, attainments and achievements to human endeavour and human intelligence. A man and only a man can become a Buddha. Every man has within himself the potentiality of becoming a Buddha, if he so wills it and endeavours. We can call the Buddha a man *par excellence*. He was so perfect in his 'human-ness' that he came to be regarded later in popular religion almost as 'super-human'.

Man's position, according to Buddhism, is supreme. Man is his own master, and there is no higher being or power that sits in judgment over his destiny.

'One is one's own refuge, who else could be the refuge?'[1] said the Buddha. He admonished his disciples to 'be a refuge to themselves', and never to seek refuge in or help from anybody else.[2] He taught, encouraged and stimulated each person to develop himself and to work out his own emancipation, for man has the power to liberate himself from all bondage through his own personal effort and intelligence. The Buddha says: 'You should do your work, for the Tathāgatas[3] only teach the way.'[4] If the Buddha is to be called a 'saviour' at all, it is only in the sense that he

[1]Dhp. XII 4.

[2]D II (Colombo, 1929), p. 62 (*Mahāparinibbāna-sutta*).

[3]*Tathāgata* lit. means 'One who has come to Truth', i.e., 'One who has discovered Truth'. This is the term usually used by the Buddha referring to himself and to the Buddhas in general.

[4]Dhp. XX 4.

discovered and showed the Path to Liberation, Nirvāṇa. But we must tread the Path ourselves.

It is on this principle of individual responsibility that the Buddha allows freedom to his disciples. In the *Mahāparinibbāna-sutta* the Buddha says that he never thought of controlling the *Sangha* (Order of Monks)[1], nor did he want the *Sangha* to depend on him. He said that there was no esoteric doctrine in his teaching, nothing hidden in the 'closed-fist of the teacher' (*ācariya-muṭṭhi*), or to put it in other words, there never was anything 'up his sleeve'.[2]

The freedom of thought allowed by the Buddha is unheard of elsewhere in the history of religions. This freedom is necessary because, according to the Buddha, man's emancipation depends on his own realization of Truth, and not on the benevolent grace of a god or any external power as a reward for his obedient good behaviour.

The Buddha once visited a small town called Kesaputta in the kingdom of Kosala. The inhabitants of this town were known by the common name Kālāma. When they heard that the Buddha was in their town, the Kālāmas paid him a visit, and told him:

'Sir, there are some recluses and brāhmaṇas who visit Kesaputta. They explain and illumine only their own doctrines, and despise, condemn and spurn others' doctrines. Then come other recluses and brāhmaṇas, and they, too, in their turn, explain and illumine only their own doctrines, and despise, condemn and spurn others' doctrines. But, for us, Sir, we have always doubt and perplexity as to who among these venerable recluses and brāhmaṇas spoke the truth, and who spoke falsehood.'

Then the Buddha gave them this advice, unique in the history of religions:

'Yes, Kālāmas, it is proper that you have doubt, that you have perplexity, for a doubt has arisen in a matter which is doubtful. Now, look you Kālāmas, do not be led by reports, or tradition, or hearsay. Be not led by the authority of religious texts, nor by mere logic or inference, nor by considering appearances, nor by the delight in speculative opinions, nor by seeming possibilities,

[1] *Sangha* lit. means 'Community'. But in Buddhism this term denotes 'The Community of Buddhist monks' which is the Order of Monks. Buddha, *Dhamma* (Teaching) and *Sangha* (Order) are known as *Tisaraṇa* 'Three Refuges' or *Tiratana* (Sanskrit *Triratna*) 'Triple-Gem'.

[2] D II (Colombo, 1929), p. 62.

nor by the idea: 'this is our teacher'. But, O Kālāmas, when you know for yourselves that certain things are unwholesome (*akusala*), and wrong, and bad, then give them up . . . And when you know for yourselves that certain things are wholesome (*kusala*) and good, then accept them and follow them.'[1]

The Buddha went even further. He told the bhikkhus that a disciple should examine even the Tathāgata (Buddha) himself, so that he (the disciple) might be fully convinced of the true value of the teacher whom he followed.[2]

According to the Buddha's teaching, doubt (*vicikicchā*) is one of the five Hindrances (*nīvaraṇa*)[3] to the clear understanding of Truth and to spiritual progress (or for that matter to any progress). Doubt, however, is not a 'sin', because there are no articles of faith in Buddhism. In fact there is no 'sin' in Buddhism, as sin is understood in some religions. The root of all evil is ignorance (*avijjā*) and false views (*micchā diṭṭhi*). It is an undeniable fact that as long as there is doubt, perplexity, wavering, no progress is possible. It is also equally undeniable that there must be doubt as long as one does not understand or see clearly. But in order to progress further it is absolutely necessary to get rid of doubt. To get rid of doubt one has to see clearly.

There is no point in saying that one should not doubt or one should believe. Just to say 'I believe' does not mean that you understand and see. When a student works on a mathematical problem, he comes to a stage beyond which he does not know how to proceed, and where he is in doubt and perplexity. As long as he has this doubt, he cannot proceed. If he wants to proceed, he must resolve this doubt. And there are ways of resolving that doubt. Just to say 'I believe', or 'I do not doubt' will certainly not solve the problem. To force oneself to believe and to accept a thing without understanding is political, and not spiritual or intellectual.

The Buddha was always eager to dispel doubt. Even just a few minutes before his death, he requested his disciples several times to ask him if they had any doubts about his teaching, and not to

[1] A (Colombo, 1929), p. 115.

[2] *Vīmaṃsaka-sutta*, no. 47 of M.

[3] The Five Hindrances are: (1) Sensuous Lust, (2) Ill-will, (3) Physical and mental torpor and languour, (4) Restlessness and Worry, (5) Doubt.

feel sorry later that they could not clear those doubts. But the disciples were silent. What he said then was touching: 'If it is through respect for the Teacher that you do not ask anything, let even one of you inform his friend' (i.e., let one tell his friend so that the latter may ask the question on the other's behalf).[1]

Not only the freedom of thought, but also the tolerance allowed by the Buddha is astonishing to the student of the history of religions. Once in Nālandā a prominent and wealthy householder named Upāli, a well-known lay disciple of Nigaṇṭha Nātaputta (Jaina Mahāvīra), was expressly sent by Mahāvīra himself to meet the Buddha and defeat him in argument on certain points in the theory of Karma, because the Buddha's views on the subject were different from those of Mahāvīra.[2] Quite contrary to expectations, Upāli, at the end of the discussion, was convinced that the views of the Buddha were right and those of his master were wrong. So he begged the Buddha to accept him as one of his lay disciples (*Upāsaka*). But the Buddha asked him to reconsider it, and not to be in a hurry, for 'considering carefully is good for well-known men like you'. When Upāli expressed his desire again, the Buddha requested him to continue to respect and support his old religious teachers as he used to.[3]

In the third century B.C., the great Buddhist Emperor Asoka of India, following this noble example of tolerance and understanding, honoured and supported all other religions in his vast empire. In one of his Edicts carved on rock, the original of which one may read even today, the Emperor declared:

'One should not honour only one's own religion and condemn the religions of others, but one should honour others' religions for this or that reason. So doing, one helps one's own religion to grow and renders service to the religions of others too. In acting otherwise one digs the grave of one's own religion and also does harm to other religions. Whosoever honours his own religion and condemns other religions, does so indeed through devotion to his own religion, thinking "I will glorify my own religion". But on the contrary, in so doing he injures his own religion more gravely.

[1] D II (Colombo, 1929), p. 95; A (Colombo, 1929), p. 239.

[2] Mahāvīra, founder of Jainism, was a contemporary of the Buddha, and was probably a few years older than the Buddha.

[3] *Upāli-sutta*, no. 56 of M.

So concord is good: Let all listen, and be willing to listen to the doctrines professed by others'.[1]

We should add here that this spirit of sympathetic understanding should be applied today not only in the matter of religious doctrine, but elsewhere as well.

This spirit of tolerance and understanding has been from the beginning one of the most cherished ideals of Buddhist culture and civilization. That is why there is not a single example of persecution or the shedding of a drop of blood in converting people to Buddhism, or in its propagation during its long history of 2500 years. It spread peacefully all over the continent of Asia, having more than 500 million adherents today. Violence in any form, under any pretext whatsoever, is absolutely against the teaching of the Buddha.

The question has often been asked: Is Buddhism a religion or a philosophy? It does not matter what you call it. Buddhism remains what it is whatever label you may put on it. The label is immaterial. Even the label 'Buddhism' which we give to the teaching of the Buddha is of little importance. The name one gives it is inessential.

> What's in a name? That which we call a rose,
> By any other name would smell as sweet.

In the same way Truth needs no label: it is neither Buddhist, Christian, Hindu nor Moslem. It is not the monopoly of anybody. Sectarian labels are a hindrance to the independent understanding of Truth, and they produce harmful prejudices in men's minds.

This is true not only in intellectual and spiritual matters, but also in human relations. When, for instance, we meet a man, we do not look on him as a human being, but we put a label on him, such as English, French, German, American, or Jew, and regard him with all the prejudices associated with that label in our mind. Yet he may be completely free from those attributes which we have put on him.

People are so fond of discriminative labels that they even go to the length of putting them on human qualities and emotions common to all. So they talk of different 'brands' of charity, as for example, of Buddhist charity or Christian charity, and look down

[1]Rock Edict, XII.

upon other 'brands' of charity. But charity cannot be sectarian; it is neither Christian, Buddhist, Hindu nor Moslem. The love of a mother for her child is neither Buddhist nor Christian: it is mother love. Human qualities and emotions like love, charity, compassion, tolerance, patience, friendship, desire, hatred, ill-will, ignorance, conceit, etc., need no sectarian labels; they belong to no particular religions.

To the seeker after Truth it is immaterial from where an idea comes. The source and development of an idea is a matter for the academic. In fact, in order to understand Truth, it is not necessary even to know whether the teaching comes from the Buddha, or from anyone else. What is essential is seeing the thing, understanding it. There is an important story in the *Majjhima-nikāya* (*sutta* no. 140) which illustrates this.

The Buddha once spent a night in a potter's shed. In the same shed there was a young recluse who had arrived there earlier.[1] They did not know each other. The Buddha observed the recluse, and thought to himself: 'Pleasant are the ways of this young man. It would be good if I should ask about him'. So the Buddha asked him: 'O bhikkhu,[2] in whose name have you left home? Or who is your master? Or whose doctrine do you like?'

'O friend,' answered the young man, 'there is the recluse Gotama, a Sakyan scion, who left the Sakya-family to become a recluse. There is high repute abroad of him that he is an Arahant, a Fully-Enlightened One. In the name of that Blessed One I have become a recluse. He is my Master, and I like his doctrine'.

'Where does that Blessed One, the Arahant, the Fully-Enlightened One live at the present time?'

'In the countries to the north, friend, there is a city called

[1]In India potters' sheds are spacious, and quiet. References are made in the Pali texts to ascetics and recluses, as well as to the Buddha himself, spending a night in a potter's shed during their wanderings.

[2]It is interesting to note here that the Buddha addresses this recluse as *Bhikkhu*, which term is used for Buddhist monks. In the sequel it will be seen that he was not a bhikkhu, not a member of the Order of the Sangha, for he asked the Buddha to admit him into the Order. Perhaps in the days of the Buddha the term 'bhikkhu' was used at times even for other ascetics indiscriminately, or the Buddha was not very strict in the use of the term. Bhikkhu means 'mendicant' 'one who begs food', and perhaps it was used here in its literal and original sense. But today the term 'bhikkhu' is used only of Buddhist monks, especially in Theravāda countries like Ceylon, Burma, Thailand, Cambodia, and in Chittagong.

Sāvatthi. It is there that that Blessed One, the Arahant, the Fully-Enlightened One, is now living.'

'Have you ever seen him, that Blessed One? Would you recognize him if you saw him?'

'I have never seen that Blessed One. Nor should I recognize him if I saw him.'

The Buddha realized that it was in his name that this unknown young man had left home and become a recluse. But without divulging his own identity, he said: 'O bhikkhu, I will teach you the doctrine. Listen and pay attention. I will speak.'

'Very well, friend,' said the young man in assent.

Then the Buddha delivered to this young man a most remarkable discourse explaining Truth (the gist of which is given later).[1]

It was only at the end of the discourse that this young recluse, whose name was Pukkusāti, realized that the person who spoke to him was the Buddha himself. So he got up, went before the Buddha, bowed down at the feet of the Master, and apologized to him for calling him 'friend'[2] unknowingly. He then begged the Buddha to ordain him and admit him into the Order of the *Sangha*.

The Buddha asked him whether he had the alms-bowl and the robes ready. (A bhikkhu must have three robes and the alms-bowl for begging food.) When Pukkusāti replied in the negative, the Buddha said that the Tathāgatas would not ordain a person unless the alms-bowl and the robes were ready. So Pukkusāti went out in search of an alms-bowl and robes, but was unfortunately savaged by a cow and died.[3]

Later, when this sad news reached the Buddha, he announced that Pukkusāti was a wise man, who had already seen Truth, and

[1]In the chapter on the third Noble Truth, see p. 38.

[2]The term used is *Āvuso* which means friend. It is a respectful term of address among equals. But disciples never use this term addressing the Buddha. Instead they use the term *Bhante* which approximately means 'Sir' or 'Lord'. At the time of the Buddha, the members of his Order of Monks (Sangha) addressed one another as *Āvuso* 'Friend'. But before his death the Buddha instructed younger monks to address their elders as *Bhante* 'Sir' or *Āyasmā* 'Venerable'. But elders should address the younger members by name, or as *Āvuso* 'Friend'. (D II Colombo, 1929, p. 95). This practice is continued up to the present day in the Sangha.

[3]It is well-known that cows in India roam about the streets. From this reference it seems that the tradition is very old. But generally these cows are docile and not savage or dangerous.

attained the penultimate stage in the realization of Nirvāṇa, and that he was born in a realm where he would become an Arahant[1] and finally pass away, never to return to this world again[2].

From this story it is quite clear that when Pukkusāti listened to the Buddha and understood his teaching, he did not know who was speaking to him, or whose teaching it was. He saw Truth. If the medicine is good, the disease will be cured. It is not necessary to know who prepared it, or where it came from.

Almost all religions are built on faith—rather 'blind' faith it would seem. But in Buddhism emphasis is laid on 'seeing', knowing, understanding, and not on faith, or belief. In Buddhist texts there is a word *saddhā* (Skt. *śraddhā*) which is usually translated as 'faith' or 'belief'. But *saddhā* is not 'faith' as such, but rather 'confidence' born out of conviction. In popular Buddhism and also in ordinary usage in the texts the word *saddhā*, it must be admitted, has an element of 'faith' in the sense that it signifies devotion to the Buddha, the *Dhamma* (Teaching) and the *Sangha* (The Order).

According to Asanga, the great Buddhist philosopher of the 4th century A.C., *śraddhā* has three aspects: (1) full and firm conviction that a thing is, (2) serene joy at good qualities, and (3) aspiration or wish to achieve an object in view.[3]

However you put it, faith or belief as understood by most religions has little to do with Buddhism.[4]

The question of belief arises when there is no seeing—seeing in every sense of the word. The moment you see, the question of belief disappears. If I tell you that I have a gem hidden in the folded palm of my hand, the question of belief arises because you

[1]An *Arahant* is a person who has liberated himself from all defilements and impurities such as desire, hatred, ill-will, ignorance, pride, conceit, etc. He has attained the fourth or the highest and ultimate stage in the realization of Nirvāṇa, and is full of wisdom, compassion and such pure and noble qualities. Pukkusāti had attained at the moment only the third stage which is technically called *Anāgāmi* 'Never-Returner'. The second stage is called *Sakadāgāmi* 'Once-Returner' and the first stage is called *Sotāpanna* 'Stream-Entrant'.

[2]Karl Gjellerup's *The Pilgrim Kamanita* seems to have been inspired by this story of Pukkusāti.

[3]Abhisamuc, p. 6.

[4]*The Role of the Miracle in Early Pali Literature* by Edith Ludowyk-Gyomroi takes up this subject. Unfortunately this Ph.D. thesis is not yet published. On the same subject see an article by the same author in the University of Ceylon Review, Vol. 1, No. 1 (April, 1943), p. 74 ff.

do not see it yourself. But if I unclench my fist and show you the gem, then you see it for yourself, and the question of belief does not arise. So the phrase in ancient Buddhist texts reads: 'Realizing, as one sees a gem (or a myrobalan fruit) in the palm'.

A disciple of the Buddha named Musīla tells another monk: 'Friend Saviṭṭha, without devotion, faith or belief,[1] without liking or inclination, without hearsay or tradition, without considering apparent reasons, without delight in the speculations of opinions, I know and see that the cessation of becoming is Nirvāṇa.'[2]

And the Buddha says: 'O bhikkhus, I say that the destruction of defilement and impurities is (meant) for a person who knows and who sees, and not for a person who does not know and does not see.'[3]

It is always a question of knowing and seeing, and not that of believing. The teaching of the Buddha is qualified as *ehi-passika*, inviting you to 'come and see', but not to come and believe.

The expressions used everywhere in Buddhist texts referring to persons who realized Truth are: 'The dustless and stainless Eye of Truth (*Dhamma-cakkhu*) has arisen.' 'He has seen Truth, has attained Truth, has known Truth, has penetrated into Truth, has crossed over doubt, is without wavering.' 'Thus with right wisdom he sees it as it is (*yathā bhūtaṃ*)'.[4] With reference to his own Enlightenment the Buddha said: 'The eye was born, knowledge was born, wisdom was born, science was born, light was born.'[5] It is always seeing through knowledge or wisdom (*ñāṇa-dassana*), and not believing through faith.

This was more and more appreciated at a time when Brāhmaṇic orthodoxy intolerantly insisted on believing and accepting their tradition and authority as the only Truth without question. Once a group of learned and well-known Brahmins went to see the Buddha and had a long discussion with him. One of the group, a Brahmin youth of 16 years of age, named Kāpaṭhika, considered

[1]Here the word *saddhā* is used in its ordinary popular sense of 'devotion, faith, belief'.

[2]S II (PTS.), p. 117.

[3]*Ibid.* III, p. 152.

[4]E.g. S V, (PTS), p. 423; III, p. 103; M III (PTS), p. 19.

[5]S V (PTS), p. 422.

by them all to be an exceptionally brilliant mind, put a question to the Buddha:[1]

'Venerable Gotama, there are the ancient holy scriptures of the Brahmins handed down along the line by unbroken oral tradition of texts. With regard to them, Brahmins come to the absolute conclusion :"This alone is Truth, and everything else is false". Now, what does the Venerable Gotama say about this?'

The Buddha inquired: 'Among Brahmins is there any one single Brahmin who claims that he personally knows and sees that "This alone is Truth, and everything else is false."?'

The young man was frank, and said: 'No'.

'Then, is there any one single teacher, or a teacher of teachers of Brahmins back to the seventh generation, or even any one of those original authors of those scriptures, who claims that he knows and he sees: "This alone is Truth, and everything else is false"?'

'No.'

'Then, it is like a line of blind men, each holding on to the preceding one; the first one does not see, the middle one also does not see, the last one also does not see. Thus, it seems to me that the state of the Brahmins is like that of a line of blind men.'

Then the Buddha gave advice of extreme importance to the group of Brahmins: 'It is not proper for a wise man who maintains (lit. protects) truth to come to the conclusion: "This alone is Truth, and everything else is false".'

Asked by the young Brahmin to explain the idea of maintaining or protecting truth, the Buddha said: 'A man has a faith. If he says "This is my faith", so far he maintains truth. But by that he cannot proceed to the absolute conclusion: "This alone is Truth, and everything else is false".' In other words, a man may believe what he likes, and he may say 'I believe this'. So far he respects truth. But because of his belief or faith, he should not say that what he believes is alone the Truth, and everything else is false.

The Buddha says: 'To be attached to one thing (to a certain view) and to look down upon other things (views) as inferior—this the wise men call a fetter.'[2]

[1] *Caṅkī-sutta,* no. 95 of M.
[2] Sn (PTS), p. 151 (v. 798).

Once the Buddha explained[1] the doctrine of cause and effect to his disciples, and they said that they saw it and understood it clearly. Then the Buddha said:

'O bhikkhus, even this view, which is so pure and so clear, if you cling to it, if you fondle it, if you treasure it, if you are attached to it, then you do not understand that the teaching is similar to a raft, which is for crossing over, and not for getting hold of.'[2]

Elsewhere the Buddha explains this famous simile in which his teaching is compared to a raft for crossing over, and not for getting hold of and carrying on one's back:

'O bhikkhus, a man is on a journey. He comes to a vast stretch of water. On this side the shore is dangerous, but on the other it is safe and without danger. No boat goes to the other shore which is safe and without danger, nor is there any bridge for crossing over. He says to himself: "This sea of water is vast, and the shore on this side is full of danger; but on the other shore it is safe and without danger. No boat goes to the other side, nor is there a bridge for crossing over. It would be good therefore if I would gather grass, wood, branches and leaves to make a raft, and with the help of the raft cross over safely to the other side, exerting myself with my hands and feet". Then that man, O bhikkhus, gathers grass, wood, branches and leaves and makes a raft, and with the help of that raft crosses over safely to the other side, exerting himself with his hands and feet. Having crossed over and got to the other side, he thinks: "This raft was of great help to me. With its aid I have crossed safely over to this side, exerting myself with my hands and feet. It would be good if I carry this raft on my head or on my back wherever I go".

'What do you think, O bhikkhus? if he acted in this way would that man be acting properly with regard to the raft?' "No, Sir". 'In which way then would he be acting properly with regard to the raft? Having crossed and gone over to the other side, suppose that man should think: "This raft was a great help to me. With its aid I have crossed safely over to this side, exerting myself with my hands and feet. It would be good if I beached this raft on the shore, or moored it and left it afloat, and then went on my way

[1]In the *Mahātaṇhāsaṅkhaya-sutta,* no. 38 of M.

[2]M I (PTS), p. 260.

wherever it may be". Acting in this way would that man act properly with regard to that raft.

'In the same manner, O bhikkhus, I have taught a doctrine similar to a raft—it is for crossing over, and not for carrying (lit. getting hold of). You, O bhikkhus, who understand that the teaching is similar to a raft, should give up even good things (*dhamma*); how much more then should you give up evil things (*adhamma*).'[1]

From this parable it is quite clear that the Buddha's teaching is meant to carry man to safety, peace, happiness, tranquility, the attainment of *Nirvāṇa*. The whole doctrine taught by the Buddha leads to this end. He did not say things just to satisfy intellectual curiosity. He was a practical teacher and taught only those things which would bring peace and happiness to man.

The Buddha was once staying in a Siṃsapa forest in Kosambi (near Allahabad). He took a few leaves into his hand, and asked his disciples: 'What do you think, O bhikkus? Which is more? These few leaves in my hand or the leaves in the forest over here?'

'Sir, very few are the leaves in the hand of the Blessed One, but indeed the leaves in the Siṃsapa forest over here are very much more abundant.'

'Even so, bhiḳkhus, of what I have known I have told you only a little, what I have not told you is very much more. And why have I not told you (those things)? Because that is not useful . . . not leading to *Nirvāṇa*. That is why I have not told you those things.'[2]

It is futile, as some scholars vainly try to do, for us to speculate on what the Buddha knew but did not tell us.

The Buddha was not interested in discussing unnecessary metaphysical questions which are purely speculative and which create imaginary problems. He considered them as a 'wilderness of opinions'. It seems that there were some among his own disciples who did not appreciate this attitude of his. For, we have

[1]M I (PTS), pp. 134-135. *Dhamma* here, according to the Commentary, means high spiritual attainments as well as pure views and ideas. Attachment even to these, however high and pure they may be, should be given up; how much more then should it be with regard to evil and bad things. MA II (PTS), p.109.

[2]S V (PTS), p. 437.

the example of one of them, Māluṅkyaputta by name, who put to the Buddha ten well-known classical questions on metaphysical problems and demanded answers.[1]

One day Māluṅkyaputta got up from his afternoon meditation, went to the Buddha, saluted him, sat on one side and said:

'Sir, when I was all alone meditating, this thought occurred to me: There are these problems unexplained, put aside and rejected by the Blessed One. Namely, (1) is the universe eternal or (2) is it not eternal, (3) is the universe finite or (4) is it infinite, (5) is soul the same as body or (6) is soul one thing and body another thing, (7) does the Tathāgata exist after death, or (8) does he not exist after death, or (9) does he both (at the same time) exist and not exist after death, or (10) does he both (at the same time) not exist and not not-exist. These problems the Blessed One does not explain to me. This (attitude) does not please me, I do not appreciate it. I will go to the Blessed One and ask him about this matter. If the Blessed One explains them to me, then I will continue to follow the holy life under him. If he does not explain them, I will leave the Order and go away. If the Blessed One knows that the universe is eternal, let him explain it to me so. If the Blessed One knows that the universe is not eternal, let him say so. If the Blessed One does not know whether the universe is eternal or not, etc., then for a person who does not know, it is straightforward to say "I do not know, I do not see".'

The Buddha's reply to Māluṅkyaputta should do good to many millions in the world today who are wasting valuable time on such metaphysical questions and unnecessarily disturbing their peace of mind:

'Did I ever tell you, Māluṅkyaputta, "Come, Māluṅkyaputta, lead the holy life under me, I will explain these questions to you?"'

'No, Sir.'

'Then, Māluṅkyaputta, even you, did you tell me: "Sir, I will lead the holy life under the Blessed One, and the Blessed One will explain these questions to me"?'

'No, Sir.'

'Even now, Māluṅkyaputta, I do not tell you: "Come and lead the holy life under me, I will explain these questions to you".

[1] *Cūla-Māluṅkya-sutta,* no. 63 of M.

And you do not tell me either: "Sir, I will lead the holy life under the Blessed One, and he will explain these questions to me". Under these circumstances, you foolish one, who refuses whom?[1]

'Māluṅkyaputta, if anyone says: "I will not lead the holy life under the Blessed One until he explains these questions, he may die with these questions unanswered by the Tathāgata. Suppose Māluṅkyaputta, a man is wounded by a poisoned arrow, and his friends and relatives bring him to a surgeon. Suppose the man should then say: "I will not let this arrow be taken out until I know who shot me; whether he is a Kṣatriya (of the warrior caste) or a Brāhmaṇa (of the priestly caste) or a Vaiśya (of the trading and agricultural caste) or a Śūdra (of the low caste); what his name and family may be; whether he is tall, short, or of medium stature; whether his complexion is black, brown, or golden; from which village, town or city he comes. I will not let this arrow be taken out until I know the kind of bow with which I was shot; the kind of bowstring used; the type of arrow; what sort of feather was used on the arrow and with what kind of material the point of the arrow was made. Māluṅkyaputta, that man would die without knowing any of these things. Even so, Māluṅkyaputta, if anyone says "I will not follow the holy life under the Blessed One until he answers these questions such as whether the universe is eternal or not, etc., he would die with these questions unanswered by the Tathāgata."

Then the Buddha explains to Māluṅkyaputta that the holy life does not depend on these views. Whatever opinion one may have about these problems, there is birth, old age, decay, death, sorrow, lamentation, pain, grief, distress, "the Cessation of which (i.e. *Nirvāṇa*) I declare in this very life."

'Therefore, Māluṅkyaputta, bear in mind what I have explained as explained, and what I have not explained as unexplained. What are the things that I have not explained? Whether the universe is eternal or not, etc., (those 10 opinions) I have not explained. Why, Māluṅkyaputta, have I not explained them? Because it is not useful, it is not fundamentally connected with the spiritual holy life, is not conducive to aversion, detachment, cessation, tranquility, deep penetration, full realization, *Nirvāṇa*. That is why I have not told you about them.

[1]i.e. both are free and neither is under obligation to the other.

'Then, what, Māluṅkyaputta, have I explained? I have explained *dukkha*, the arising of *dukkha*, the cessation of *dukkha*, and the way leading to the cessation of *dukkha*.[1] Why, Māluṅkyaputta, have I explained them? Because it is useful, is fundamentally connected with the spiritual holy life, is conducive to aversion, detachment, cessation, tranquility, deep penetration, full realization, Nirvāṇa. Therefore I have explained them.'[2]

Let us now examine the Four Noble Truths which the Buddha told Māluṅkyaputta he had explained.

[1]These Four Noble Truths are explained in the next four chapters.

[2]It seems that this advice of the Buddha had the desired effect on Māluṅkyaputta, because elsewhere he is reported to have approached the Buddha again for instruction, following which he became an Arahant. A (Colombo, 1929), pp. 345-346.

CHAPTER II

The Four Noble Truths

THE FIRST NOBLE TRUTH: *DUKKHA*

The heart of the Buddha's teaching lies in the Four Noble Truths (*Cattāri Ariyasaccāni*) which he expounded in his very first sermon[1] to his old colleagues, the five ascetics, at Isipatana (modern Sarnath) near Benares. In this sermon, as we have it in the original texts, these four Truths are given briefly. But there are innumerable places in the early Buddhist scriptures where they are explained again and again, with greater detail and in different ways. If we study the Four Noble Truths with the help of these references and explanations, we get a fairly good and accurate account of the essential teachings of the Buddha according to the original texts.

The Four Noble Truths are:

1. *Dukkha*[2]
2. *Samudaya*, the arising or origin of *dukkha*,
3. *Nirodha,* the cessation of *dukkha,*
4. *Magga,* the way leading to the cessation of *dukkha*.

THE FIRST NOBLE TRUTH: *DUKKHA*

The First Noble Truth (*Dukkha-ariyasacca*) is generally translated by almost all scholars as 'The Noble Truth of Suffering', and it is interpreted to mean that life according to Buddhism is nothing but suffering and pain. Both translation and interpretation are highly unsatisfactory and misleading. It is because of this limited, free and easy translation, and its superficial interpretation, that many people have been misled into regarding Buddhism as pessimistic.

[1] *Dhammacakkappavattana-sutta* 'Setting in Motion the Wheel of Truth'. Mhvg. (Alutgama, 1922), p. 9 ff; S V (PTS). p. 420 ff.

[2] I do not wish to give an equivalent in English for this term for reasons given below.

I. The bust of the Buddha—from Thailand

II. The head of the Buddha—from Polonnaruva, Ceylon

First of all, Buddhism is neither pessimistic nor optimistic. If anything at all, it is realistic, for it takes a realistic view of life and of the world. It looks at things objectively (*yathābhūtaṃ*). It does not falsely lull you into living in a fool's paradise, nor does it frighten and agonize you with all kinds of imaginary fears and sins. It tells you exactly and objectively what you are and what the world around you is, and shows you the way to perfect freedom, peace, tranquility and happiness.

One physician may gravely exaggerate an illness and give up hope altogether. Another may ignorantly declare that there is no illness and that no treatment is necessary, thus deceiving the patient with a false consolation. You may call the first one pessimistic and the second optimistic. Both are equally dangerous. But a third physician diagnoses the symptoms correctly, understands the cause and the nature of the illness, sees clearly that it can be cured, and courageously administers a course of treatment, thus saving his patient. The Buddha is like the last physician. He is the wise and scientific doctor for the ills of the world (*Bhisakka* or *Bhaiṣajya-guru*).

It is true that the Pali word *dukkha* (or Sanskrit *duḥkha*) in ordinary usage means 'suffering', 'pain', 'sorrow' or 'misery', as opposed to the word *sukha* meaning 'happiness', 'comfort' or 'ease'. But the term *dukkha* as the First Noble Truth, which represents the Buddha's view of life and the world, has a deeper philosophical meaning and connotes enormously wider senses. It is admitted that the term *dukkha* in the First Noble Truth contains, quite obviously, the ordinary meaning of 'suffering', but in addition it also includes deeper ideas such as 'imperfection', 'impermanence', 'emptiness', 'insubstantiality'. It is difficult therefore to find one word to embrace the whole conception of the term *dukkha* as the First Noble Truth, and so it is better to leave it untranslated, than to give an inadequate and wrong idea of it by conveniently translating it as 'suffering' or 'pain'.

The Buddha does not deny happiness in life when he says there is suffering. On the contrary he admits different forms of happiness, both material and spiritual, for laymen as well as for monks. In the *Aṅguttara-nikāya*, one of the five original Collections in Pāli containing the Buddha's discourses, there is a list of happinesses (*sukhāni*), such as the happiness of family life and the happiness of the life of a recluse, the happiness of sense pleasures and the happiness of renunciation, the happiness of attachment and the happiness of detachment, physical happiness and mental happiness etc.[1] But all these are included in *dukkha*. Even the very pure spiritual states of *dhyāna* (*recueillement* or trance) attained by the practice of higher meditation, free from even a shadow of suffering in the accepted sense of the word, states which may be described as unmixed happiness, as well as the state of *dhyāna* which is free from sensations both pleasant (*sukha*) and unpleasant (*dukkha*) and is only pure equanimity and awareness—even these very high spiritual states are included in *dukkha*. In one of the *suttas* of the *Majjhima-nikāya*, (again one of the five original Collections), after praising the spiritual happiness of these *dhyānas*, the Buddha says that they are 'impermanent, *dukkha*, and subject to change' (*aniccā dukkhā vipariṇāmadhammā*).[2] Notice that the word *dukkha* is explicitly used. It is *dukkha*, not because there is 'suffering' in the ordinary sense of the word, but because 'whatever is impermanent is *dukkha*' (*yad aniccaṃ taṃ dukkhaṃ*).

The Buddha was realistic and objective. He says, with regard to life and the enjoyment of sense-pleasures, that one should clearly understand three things: (1) attraction or enjoyment (*assāda*), (2) evil consequence or danger or unsatisfactoriness (*ādīnava*), and (3) freedom or liberation (*nissaraṇa*).[3] When you see a pleasant, charming and beautiful person, you like him (or her), you are attracted, you enjoy seeing that person again and again, you derive pleasure and satisfaction from that person. This is enjoyment (*assāda*). It is a fact of experience. But this enjoyment is not permanent, just as that person and all his (or her) attractions are not permanent either. When the situation changes, when you cannot see that person, when you are deprived of this enjoyment, you become sad, you may become unreasonable and unbalanced, you may even behave foolishly. This is the evil, unsatisfactory and dangerous side of the picture (*ādīnava*). This, too, is a fact of experience. Now if you have no attachment to the person, if you are completely detached, that is freedom, liberation

[1] A (Colombo, 1929), p. 49.
[2] *Mahādukkhakkhandha-sutta,* M I (PTS), p. 90.
[3] M I (PTS), p. 85 ff.; S III (PTS), p. 27 ff.

(*nissaraṇa*). These three things are true with regard to all enjoyment in life.

From this it is evident that it is no question of pessimism or optimism, but that we must take account of the pleasures of life as well as of its pains and sorrows, and also of freedom from them, in order to understand life completely and objectively. Only then is true liberation possible. Regarding this question the Buddha says:

'O bhikkhus, if any recluses or brāhmaṇas do not understand objectively in this way that the enjoyment of sense-pleasures is enjoyment, that their unsatisfactoriness is unsatisfactoriness, that liberation from them is liberation, then it is not possible that they themselves will certainly understand the desire for sense pleasures completely, or that they will be able to instruct another person to that end, or that the person following their instruction will completely understand the desire for sense-pleasures. But, O bhikkhus, if any recluses or brāhmaṇas understand objectively in this way that the enjoyment of sense-pleasures is enjoyment, that their unsatisfactoriness is unsatisfactoriness, that liberation from them is liberation, then it is possible that they themselves will certainly understand the desire for sense-pleasures completely, and that they will be able to instruct another person to that end, and that that person following their instruction will completely understand the desire for sense-pleasures.'[1]

The conception of *dukkha* may be viewed from three aspects: (1) *dukkha* as ordinary suffering (*dukkha-dukkha*), (2) *dukkha* as produced by change (*vipariṇāma-dukkha*) and (3) *dukkha* as conditioned states (*saṃkhāra-dukkha*).[2]

All kinds of suffering in life like birth, old age, sickness, death, association with unpleasant persons and conditions, separation from beloved ones and pleasant conditions, not getting what one desires, grief, lamentation, distress—all such forms of physical and mental suffering, which are universally accepted as suffering or pain, are included in *dukkha* as ordinary suffering (*dukkha-dukkha*).

[1]M I (PTS), p. 87.
[2]Vism (PTS), p. 499; Abhisamuc, p. 38.

A happy feeling, a happy condition in life, is not permanent, not everlasting. It changes sooner or later. When it changes, it produces pain, suffering, unhappiness. This vicissitude is included in *dukkha* as suffering produced by change (*vipariṇāma-dukkha*).

It is easy to understand the two forms of suffering (*dukkha*) mentioned above. No one will dispute them. This aspect of the First Noble Truth is more popularly known because it is easy to understand. It is common experience in our daily life.

But the third form of *dukkha* as conditioned states (*saṃkhāra-dukkha*) is the most important philosophical aspect of the First Noble Truth, and it requires some analytical explanation of what we consider as a 'being', as an 'individual', or as 'I'.

What we call a 'being', or an 'individual', or 'I', according to Buddhist philosophy, is only a combination of ever-changing physical and mental forces or energies, which may be divided into five groups or aggregates (*pañcakkhandha*). The Buddha says: 'In short these five aggregates of attachment are *dukkha*'.[1] Elsewhere he distinctly defines *dukkha* as the five aggregates: 'O bhikkhus, what is *dukkha*? It should be said that it is the five aggregates of attachment'.[2] Here it should be clearly understood that *dukkha* and the five aggregates are not two different things; the five aggregates themselves are *dukkha*. We will understand this point better when we have some notion of the five aggregates which constitute the so-called 'being'. Now, what are these five?

The Five Aggregates

The first is the Aggregate of Matter (*Rūpakkhandha*). In this term 'Aggregate of Matter' are included the traditional Four Great Elements (*cattāri mahābhūtāni*), namely, solidity, fluidity, heat and motion, and also the Derivatives (*upādāya-rūpa*) of the Four Great Elements.[3] In the term 'Derivatives of Four Great Elements' are included our five material sense-organs, i.e., the faculties of eye, ear, nose, tongue, and body, and their corresponding objects in the external world, i.e., visible form, sound, odour, taste,

[1] *Saṃkhittena pañcupādānakkhandhā dukkhā.* S V (PTS), p. 421.
[2] S III (PTS), p. 158.
[3] S III (PTS), p. 59.

and tangible things, and also some thoughts or ideas or conceptions which are in the sphere of mind-objects (*dharmāyatana*)[1]. Thus the whole realm of matter, both internal and external, is included in the Aggregate of Matter.

The second is the Aggregate of Sensations (*Vedanākkhandha*). In this group are included all our sensations, pleasant or unpleasant or neutral, experienced through the contact of physical and mental organs with the external world. They are of six kinds: the sensations experienced through the contact of the eye with visible forms, ear with sounds, nose with odour, tongue with taste, body with tangible objects, and mind (which is the sixth faculty in Buddhist Philosophy) with mind-objects or thoughts or ideas.[2] All our physical and mental sensations are included in this group.

A word about what is meant by the term 'Mind' (*manas*) in Buddhist philosophy may be useful here. It should clearly be understood that mind is not spirit as opposed to matter. It should always be remembered that Buddhism does not recognize a spirit opposed to matter, as is accepted by most other systems of philosophies and religions. Mind is only a faculty or organ (*indriya*) like the eye or the ear. It can be controlled and developed like any other faculty, and the Buddha speaks quite often of the value of controlling and disciplining these six faculties. The difference between the eye and the mind as faculties is that the former senses the world of colours and visible forms, while the latter senses the world of ideas and thoughts and mental objects. We experience different fields of the world with different senses. We cannot hear colours, but we can see them. Nor can we see sounds, but we can hear them. Thus with our five physical sense-organs—eye, ear, nose, tongue, body—we experience only the world of visible forms, sounds, odours, tastes and tangible objects. But these represent only a part of the world, not the whole world. What of ideas and thoughts? They are also a part of the world. But they cannot be sensed, they cannot be conceived by the faculty of the eye, ear, nose, tongue or body. Yet they can be conceived by another faculty, which is mind. Now ideas and

[1]Abhisamuc, p. 4.
[2]S III (PTS), p. 59.

thoughts are not independent of the world experienced by these five physical sense faculties. In fact they depend on, and are conditioned by, physical experiences. Hence a person born blind cannot have ideas of colour, except through the analogy of sounds or some other things experienced through his other faculties. Ideas and thoughts which form a part of the world are thus produced and conditioned by physical experiences and are conceived by the mind. Hence mind (*manas*) is considered a sense faculty or organ (*indriya*), like the eye or the ear.

The third is the Aggregate of Perceptions (*Saññākkhandha*). Like sensations, perceptions also are of six kinds, in relation to six internal faculties and the corresponding six external objects. Like sensations, they are produced through the contact of our six faculties with the external world. It is the perceptions that recognize objects whether physical or mental.[1]

The fourth is the Aggregate of Mental Formations [2] (*Saṃkhārakkhandha*). In this group are included all volitional activities both good and bad. What is generally known as *karma* (or *kamma*) comes under this group. The Buddha's own definition of *karma* should be remembered here: 'O bhikkhus, it is volition (*cetanā*) that I call *karma*. Having willed, one acts through body, speech and mind.'[3] Volition is 'mental construction, mental activity. Its function is to direct the mind in the sphere of good, bad or neutral activities.'[4] Just like sensations and perceptions, volition is of six kinds, connected with the six internal faculties and the corresponding six objects (both physical and mental) in the external world.[5] Sensations and perceptions are not volitional actions. They do not produce karmic effects. It is only volitional actions—such as attention (*manasikāra*), will (*chanda*), determination (*adhimokkha*), confidence (*saddhā*), concentration (*samādhi*), wisdom (*paññā*), energy (*viriya*), desire (*rāga*), repugnance or hate (*paṭigha*)

[1]S III (PTS), p. 60

[2]'Mental Formations' is a term now generally used to represent the wide meaning of the word *saṃkhāra* in the list of Five Aggregates. *Saṃkhāra* in other contexts may mean anything conditioned, anything in the world, in which sense all the Five Aggregates are *saṃkhāra*.

[3]A (Colombo, 1929), p. 590—*Cetanā'haṃ bhikkhave kammaṃ vadāmi. Cetayitvā kammaṃ karoti kāyena vācā manasā.*

[4]Abhisamuc, p. 6.

[5]S III (PTS), p. 60.

ignorance (*avijjā*), conceit (*māna*), idea of self (*sakkāya-diṭṭhi*) etc. —that can produce karmic effects. There are 52 such mental activities which constitute the Aggregate of Mental Formations.

The fifth is the Aggregate of Consciousness (*Viññāṇakkhandha*).[1] Consciousness is a reaction or response which has one of the six faculties (eye, ear, nose, tongue, body and mind) as its basis, and one of the six corresponding external phenomena (visible form, sound, odour, taste, tangible things and mind-objects, i.e., an idea or thought) as its object. For instance, visual consciousness (*cakkhu-viññāṇa*) has the eye as its basis and a visible form as its object. Mental consciousness (*mano-viññāṇa*) has the mind (*manas*) as its basis and a mental object, i.e., an idea or thought (*dhamma*) as its object. So consciousness is connected with other faculties. Thus, like sensation, perception and volition, consciousness also is of six kinds, in relation to six internal faculties and corresponding six external objects.[2]

It should be clearly understood that consciousness does not recognize an object. It is only a sort of awareness—awareness of the presence of an object. When the eye comes in contact with a colour, for instance blue, visual consciousness arises which simply is awareness of the presence of a colour; but it does not recognize that it is blue. There is no recognition at this stage. It is perception (the third Aggregate discussed above) that recognizes that it is blue. The term 'visual consciousness' is a philosophical expression denoting the same idea as is conveyed by the ordinary word 'seeing'. Seeing does not mean recognizing. So are the other forms of consciousness.

It must be repeated here that according to Buddhist philosophy there is no permanent, unchanging spirit which can be considered 'Self', or 'Soul', or 'Ego', as opposed to matter, and that consciousness (*viññāṇa*) should not be taken as 'spirit' in opposition to matter. This point has to be particularly emphasized, because a wrong notion that consciousness is a sort of Self or Soul that

[1]According to Mahāyāna Buddhist philosophy the Aggregate of Consciousness has three aspects: *citta*, *manas* and *vijñāna*, and the *Ālaya-vijñāna* (popularly translated as 'Store-Consciousness') finds its place in this Aggegate. A detailed and comparative study of this subject will be found in a forthcoming work on Buddhist philosophy by the present writer.

[2]S III (PTS), p. 61.

continues as a permanent substance through life, has persisted from the earliest time to the present day.

One of the Buddha's own disciples, Sāti by name, held that the Master taught: 'It is the same consciousness that transmigrates and wanders about.' The Buddha asked him what he meant by 'consciousness'. Sāti's reply is classical: 'It is that which expresses, which feels, which experiences the results of good and bad deeds here and there'.

'To whomever, you stupid one', remonstrated the Master, 'have you heard me expounding the doctrine in this manner? Haven't I in many ways explained consciousness as arising out of conditions: that there is no arising of consciousness without conditions.' Then the Buddha went on to explain consciousness in detail: 'Consciousness is named according to whatever condition through which it arises: on account of the eye and visible forms arises a consciousness, and it is called visual consciousness; on account of the ear and sounds arises a consciousness, and it is called auditory consciousness; on account of the nose and odours arises a consciousness, and it is called olfactory consciousness; on account of the tongue and tastes arises a consciousness, and it is called gustatory consciousness; on account of the body and tangible objects arises a consciousness, and it is called tactile consciousness; on account of the mind and mind-objects (ideas and thoughts) arises a consciousness, and it is called mental consciousness.'

Then the Buddha explained it further by an illustration: A fire is named according to the material on account of which it burns. A fire may burn on account of wood, and it is called wood-fire. It may burn on account of straw, and then it is called straw-fire. So consciousness is named according to the condition through which it arises.[1]

Dwelling on this point, Buddhaghosa, the great commentator, explains: '. . . a fire that burns on account of wood burns only when there is a supply, but dies down in that very place when it (the supply) is no longer there, because then the condition has changed, but (the fire) does not cross over to splinters, etc., and

[1] *Mahātaṇhāsaṃkhaya-sutta*, M I (PTS), p. 256 ff.

become a splinter-fire and so on; even so the consciousness that arises on account of the eye and visible forms arises in that gate of sense organ (i.e., in the eye), only when there is the condition of the eye, visible forms, light and attention, but ceases then and there when it (the condition) is no more there, because then the condition has changed, but (the consciousness) does not cross over to the ear, etc., and become auditory consciousness and so on . . .'[1]

The Buddha declared in unequivocal terms that consciousness depends on matter, sensation, perception and mental formations, and that it cannot exist independently of them. He says:

'Consciousness may exist having matter as its means (*rūpupāyaṃ*), matter as its object (*rūpārammaṇaṃ*), matter as its support (*rūpa-patiṭṭhaṃ*), and seeking delight it may grow, increase and develop; or consciousness may exist having sensation as its means . . . or perception as its means . . . or mental formations as its means, mental formations as its object, mental formations as its support, and seeking delight it may grow, increase and develop.

'Were a man to say: I shall show the coming, the going, the passing away, the arising, the growth, the increase or the development of consciousness apart from matter, sensation, perception and mental formations, he would be speaking of something that does not exist.'[2]

Very briefly these are the five Aggregates. What we call a 'being', or an 'individual', or 'I', is only a convenient name or a label given to the combination of these five groups. They are all impermanent, all constantly changing. 'Whatever is impermanent is *dukkha*' (*Yad aniccaṃ taṃ dukkhaṃ*). This is the true meaning of the Buddha's words: 'In brief the five Aggregates of Attachment are *dukkha*.' They are not the same for two consecutive moments. Here A is not equal to A. They are in a flux of momentary arising and disappearing.

'O Brāhmaṇa, it is just like a mountain river, flowing far and swift, taking everything along with it; there is no moment, no instant, no second when it stops flowing, but it goes on flowing and

[1]MA II (PTS), pp. 306-307.
[2]S III (PTS), p. 58.

continuing. So Brāhmaṇa, is human life, like a mountain river.'[1] As the Buddha told Raṭṭhapāla: 'The world is in continuous flux and is impermanent.'

One thing disappears, conditioning the appearance of the next in a series of cause and effect. There is no unchanging substance in them. There is nothing behind them that can be called a permanent Self (*Ātman*), individuality, or anything that can in reality be called 'I'. Every one will agree that neither matter, nor sensation, nor perception, nor any one of those mental activities, nor consciousness can really be called 'I'.[2] But when these five physical and mental aggregates which are interdependent are working together in combination as a physio-psychological machine,[3] we get the idea of 'I'. But this is only a false idea, a mental formation, which is nothing but one of those 52 mental formations of the fourth Aggregate which we have just discussed, namely, it is the idea of self (*sakkāya-diṭṭhi*).

These five Aggregates together, which we popularly call a 'being', are *dukkha* itself (*saṃkhāra-dukkha*). There is no other 'being' or 'I', standing behind these five aggregates, who experiences *dukkha*. As Buddhaghosa says:

> 'Mere suffering exists, but no sufferer is found;
> The deeds are, but no doer is found.'[4]

There is no unmoving mover behind the movement. It is only movement. It is not correct to say that life is moving, but life is movement itself. Life and movement are not two different things. In other words, there is no thinker behind the thought. Thought itself is the thinker. If you remove the thought, there is no thinker to be found. Here we cannot fail to notice how this Buddhist view is diametrically opposed to the Cartesian *cogito ergo sum*: 'I think, therefore I am.'

Now a question may be raised whether life has a beginning.

[1]A (Colombo, 1929), p. 700. These words are attributed by the Buddha to a Teacher (*Satthā*) named Araka who was free from desires and who lived in the dim past. It is interesting to remember here the doctrine of Heraclitus (about 500 B.C.) that everything is in a state of flux, and his famous statement: 'You cannot step twice into the same river, for fresh waters are ever flowing in upon you.'

[2]The doctrine of Anatta 'No-Self' will be discussed in Chapter VI.

[3]In fact Buddhaghosa compares a 'being' to a wooden mechanism (*dāruyanta*). Vism. (PTS), pp. 594-595.

[4]Vism. (PTS), p. 513.

According to the Buddha's teaching the beginning of the life-stream of living beings is unthinkable. The believer in the creation of life by God may be astonished at this reply. But if you were to ask him 'What is the beginning of God?' he would answer without hesitation 'God has no beginning', and he is not astonished at his own reply. The Buddha says: 'O bhikkhus, this cycle of continuity (*saṃsāra*) is without a visible end, and the first beginning of beings wandering and running round, enveloped in ignorance (*avijjā*) and bound down by the fetters of thirst (desire, *taṇhā*) is not to be perceived.'[1] And further, referring to ignorance which is the main cause of the continuity of life the Buddha states: 'The first beginning of ignorance (*avijjā*) is not to be perceived in such a way as to postulate that there was no ignorance beyond a certain point.'[2] Thus it is not possible to say that there was no life beyond a certain definite point.

This in short is the meaning of the Noble Truth of *Dukkha*. It is extremely important to understand this First Noble Truth clearly because, as the Buddha says, 'he who sees *dukkha* sees also the arising of *dukkha*, sees also the cessation of *dukkha*, and sees also the path leading to the cessation of *dukkha*.'[3]

This does not at all make the life of a Buddhist melancholy or sorrowful, as some people wrongly imagine. On the contrary, a true Buddhist is the happiest of beings. He has no fears or anxieties. He is always calm and serene, and cannot be upset or dismayed by changes or calamities, because he sees things as they are. The Buddha was never melancholy or gloomy. He was described by his contemporaries as 'ever-smiling' (*mihita-pubbaṃgama*). In Buddhist painting and sculpture the Buddha is always represented with a countenance happy, serene, contented and compassionate. Never a trace of suffering or agony or pain is to be seen.[4] Buddhist art and architecture, Buddhist temples

[1]S III (PTS), pp. 178-179; III pp. 149, 151.

[2]A V (PTS), p. 113.

[3]S V (PTS), p. 437. In fact the Buddha says that he who sees any one of the Four Noble Truths sees the other three as well. These Four Noble Truths are inter-connected.

[4]There is a statue from Gandhara, and also one from Fou-Kien, China, depicting Gotama as an ascetic, emaciated, with all his ribs showing. But this was before his Enlightenment, when he was submitting himself to the rigorous ascetic practices which he condemned after he became Buddha.

never give the impression of gloom or sorrow, but produce an atmosphere of calm and serene joy.

Although there is suffering in life, a Buddhist should not be gloomy over it, should not be angry or impatient at it. One of the principal evils in life, according to Buddhism, is 'repugnance' or hatred. Repugnance (*pratigha*) is explained as 'ill-will with regard to living beings, with regard to suffering and with regard to things pertaining to suffering. Its function is to produce a basis for unhappy states and bad conduct.'[1] Thus it is wrong to be impatient at suffering. Being impatient or angry at suffering does not remove it. On the contrary, it adds a little more to one's troubles, and aggravates and exacerbates a situation already disagreeable. What is necessary is not anger or impatience, but the understanding of the question of suffering, how it comes about, and how to get rid of it, and then to work accordingly with patience, intelligence determination and energy.

There are two ancient Buddhist texts called the *Theragāthā* and *Therīgāthā* which are full of the joyful utterances of the Buddha's disciples, both male and female, who found peace and happiness in life through his teaching. The king of Kosala once told the Buddha that unlike many a disciple of other religious systems who looked haggard, coarse, pale, emaciated and unprepossessing, his disciples were 'joyful and elated (*haṭṭha-pahaṭṭha*), jubilant and exultant (*udaggudagga*), enjoying the spiritual life (*abhiratarūpa*), with faculties pleased (*pīṇitindriya*), free from anxiety (*appossukka*), serene (*pannaloma*), peaceful (*paradavutta*) and living with a gazelle's mind (*migabhūtena cetasā*), i.e., light-hearted.' The king added that he believed that this healthy disposition was due to the fact that 'these venerable ones had certainly realized the great and full significance of the Blessed One's teaching.'[2]

Buddhism is quite opposed to the melancholic, sorrowful, penitent and gloomy attitude of mind which is considered a hindrance to the realization of Truth. On the other hand, it is interesting to remember here that joy (*pīti*) is one of the seven *Bojjhaṃgas* or 'Factors of Illumination', the essential qualities to be cultivated for the realization of Nirvāṇā.[3]

[1]Abhisamic, p. 7.

[2]M II (PTS), p. 121.

[3]For these Seven Factors of Illumination see Chapter on Meditation, p. 75.

CHAPTER III

THE SECOND NOBLE TRUTH:

SAMUDAYA: 'The Arising of *Dukkha*'

The Second Noble Truth is that of the arising or origin of *dukkha* (*Dukkhasamudaya-ariyasacca*). The most popular and well-known definition of the Second Truth as found in innumerable places in the original texts runs as follows:

'It is this "thirst" (craving, *taṇhā*) which produces re-existence and re-becoming (*ponobhavikā*), and which is bound up with passionate greed (*nandīrāgasahagatā*), and which finds fresh delight now here and now there (*tatratatrābhinandinī*), namely, (1) thirst for sense-pleasures (*kāma-taṇhā*), (2) thirst for existence and becoming (*bhava-taṇhā*) and (3) thirst for non-existence (self-annihilation, *vibhava-taṇhā*).'[1]

It is this 'thirst', desire, greed, craving, manifesting itself in various ways, that gives rise to all forms of suffering and the continuity of beings. But it should not be taken as the first cause, for there is no first cause possible as, according to Buddhism, everything is relative and inter-dependent. Even this 'thirst', *taṇhā*, which is considered as the cause or origin of *dukkha*, depends for its arising (*samudaya*) on something else, which is sensation (*vedanā*),[2] and sensation arises depending on contact (*phassa*), and so on and so forth goes on the circle which is known as Conditioned Genesis (*Paṭicca-samuppāda*), which we will discuss later.[3]

So *taṇhā*, 'thirst', is not the first or the only cause of the arising of *dukkha*. But it is the most palpable and immediate cause, the 'principal thing' and the 'all-pervading thing'.[4] Hence in certain

[1] Mhvg. (Alutgama, 1922), p. 9; S V (PTS), p. 421 and *passim.*

[2] *Vedanāsamudayā taṇhāsamudayo.* M I (PTS), p. 51.

[3] See p. 53.

[4] Abhisamuc, p. 43, *prādhānyārtha, sarvatragārtha.*

places of the original Pali texts themselves the definition of *samudaya* or the origin of *dukkha* includes other defilements and impurities (*kilesā, sāsavā dhammā*), in addition to *taṇhā* 'thirst' which is always given the first place.[1] Within the necessarily limited space of our discussion, it will be sufficient if we remember that this 'thirst' has as its centre the false idea of self arising out of ignorance.

Here the term 'thirst' includes not only desire for, and attachment to, sense-pleasures, wealth and power, but also desire for, and attachment to, ideas and ideals, views, opinions, theories, conceptions and beliefs (*dhamma-taṇhā*).[2] According to the Buddha's analysis, all the troubles and strife in the world, from little personal quarrels in families to great wars between nations and countries, arise out of this selfish 'thirst'.[3] From this point of view, all economic, political and social problems are rooted in this selfish 'thirst'. Great statesmen who try to settle international disputes and talk of war and peace only in economic and political terms touch the superficialities, and never go deep into the real root of the problem. As the Buddha told Raṭṭapāla: 'The world lacks and hankers, and is enslaved to "thirst" (*taṇhādāso*).'

Every one will admit that all the evils in the world are produced by selfish desire. This is not difficult to understand. But how this desire, 'thirst', can produce re-existence and re-becoming (*ponobhavikā*) is a problem not so easy to grasp. It is here that we have to discuss the deeper philosophical side of the Second Noble Truth corresponding to the philosophical side of the First Noble Truth. Here we must have some idea about the theory of *karma* and rebirth.

There are four Nutriments (*āhāra*) in the sense of 'cause' or 'condition' necessary for the existence and continuity of beings: (1) ordinary material food (*kabaliṅkārāhāra*), (2) contact of our sense-organs (including mind) with the external world (*phassāhāra*), (3) consciousness (*viññāṇāhara*) and (4) mental volition or will (*manosañcetanāhāra*).[4]

[1] See Vibh. (PTS), p. 106 ff.

[2] M I (PTS), p. 51; S II p. 72; Vibh. p. 380.

[3] M I, p. 86.

[4] *ibid.*, p. 48.

Of these four, the last mentioned 'mental volition' is the will to live, to exist, to re-exist, to continue, to become more and more.[1] It creates the root of existence and continuity, striving forward by way of good and bad actions (*kusalākusalakamma*).[2] It is the same as 'Volition' (*cetanā*).[3] We have seen earlier[4] that volition is karma, as the Buddha himself has defined it. Referring to 'Mental volition' just mentioned above the Buddha says: 'When one understands the nutriment of mental volition one understands the three forms of 'thirst' (*taṇhā*).'[5] Thus the terms 'thirst', 'volition', 'mental volition' and 'karma' all denote the same thing: they denote the desire, the will to be, to exist, to re-exist, to become more and more, to grow more and more, to accumulate more and more. This is the cause of the arising of *dukkha*, and this is found within the Aggregate of Mental Formations, one of the Five Aggregates which constitute a being.[6]

Here is one of the most important and essential points in the Buddha's teaching. We must therefore clearly and carefully mark and remember that the cause, the germ, of the arising of *dukkha* is within *dukkha* itself, and not outside; and we must equally well remember that the cause, the germ, of the cessation of *dukkha*, of the destruction of *dukkha*, is also within *dukkha* itself, and not outside. This is what is meant by the well-known formula often found in original Pali texts: *Yaṃ kiñci samudayadhammaṃ sabbaṃ taṃ nirodhadhammaṃ* 'Whatever is of the nature of arising, all that is of the nature of cessation.'[7] A being, a thing, or a system, if it has within itself the nature of arising, the nature of coming into being, has also within itself the nature, the germ, of its own cessation and destruction. Thus *dukkha* (Five Aggregates) has within itself the nature of its own arising, and has also within

[1]It is interesting to compare this 'mental volition' with 'libido' in modern psychology.

[2]MA I (PTS), p. 210.

[3]*Manosañcetanā' ti cetanā eva vuccati.* MA I (PTS), p. 209.

[4]See above p. 22.

[5]S II (PTS), p. 100. The three forms of 'thirst' are: (1) Thirst for sense-pleasures, (2) Thirst for existence and becoming, and (3) Thirst for non-existence, as given in the definition of *samudaya* 'arising of *dukkha*' above.

[6]See above p. 22.

[7]M III (PTS) p. 280; S IV, pp. 47, 107; V, p. 423 and *passim*.

itself the nature of its own cessation. This point will be taken up again in the discussion of the Third Noble Truth, *Nirodha*.

Now, the Pali word *kamma* or the Sanskrit word *karma* (from the root *kṛ* to do) literally means 'action', 'doing'. But in the Buddhist theory of karma it has a specific meaning: it means only 'volitional action', not all action. Nor does it mean the result of karma as many people wrongly and loosely use it. In Buddhist terminology karma never means its effect; its effect is known as the 'fruit' or the 'result' of karma (*kamma-phala* or *kamma-vipāka*).

Volition may relatively be good or bad, just as a desire may relatively be good or bad. So karma may be good or bad relatively. Good karma (*kusala*) produces good effects, and bad karma (*akusala*) produces bad effects. 'Thirst', volition, karma, whether good or bad, has one force as its effect: force to continue—to continue in a good or bad direction. Whether good or bad it is relative, and is within the cycle of continuity (*saṃsāra*). An Arahant, though he acts, does not accumulate karma, because he is free from the false idea of self, free from the 'thirst' for continuity and becoming, free from all other defilements and impurities (*kilesā, sāsavā dhammā*). For him there is no rebirth.

The theory of karma should not be confused with so-called 'moral justice' or 'reward and punishment'. The idea of moral justice, or reward and punishment, arises out of the conception of a supreme being, a God, who sits in judgment, who is a law-giver and who decides what is right and wrong. The term 'justice' is ambiguous and dangerous, and in its name more harm than good is done to humanity. The theory of karma is the theory of cause and effect, of action and reaction; it is a natural law, which has nothing to do with the idea of justice or reward and punishment. Every volitional action produces its effects or results. If a good action produces good effects and a bad action bad effects, it is not justice, or reward, or punishment meted out by anybody or any power sitting in judgment on your action, but this is in virtue of its own nature, its own law. This is not difficult to understand. But what is difficult is that, according to the karma theory, the effects of a volitional action may continue to manifest themselves even in a life after death. Here we have to explain what death is according to Buddhism.

We have seen earlier that a being is nothing but a combination

III. Interior of cave temple—from Dambulla, Ceylon

IV. The Great Renunciation—Ananda Temple, Burma

V. The Buddha—from Mathura, India

VI. The Buddha—from China

of physical and mental forces or energies. What we call death is the total non-functioning of the physical body. Do all these forces and energies stop altogether with the non-functioning of the body? Buddhism says 'No'. Will, volition, desire, thirst to exist, to continue, to become more and more, is a tremendous force that moves whole lives, whole existences, that even moves the whole world. This is the greatest force, the greatest energy in the world. According to Buddhism, this force does not stop with the non-functioning of the body, which is death; but it continues manifesting itself in another form, producing re-existence which is called rebirth.

Now, another question arises: If there is no permanent, unchanging entity or substance like Self or Soul (*ātman*), what is it that can re-exist or be reborn after death? Before we go on to life after death, let us consider what this life is, and how it continues now. What we call life, as we have so often repeated, is the combination of the Five Aggregates, a combination of physical and mental energies. These are constantly changing; they do not remain the same for two consecutive moments. Every moment they are born and they die. 'When the Aggregates arise, decay and die, O bhikkhu, every moment you are born, decay and die.'[1] Thus, even now during this life time, every moment we are born and die, but we continue. If we can understand that in this life we can continue without a permanent, unchanging substance like Self or Soul, why can't we understand that those forces themselves can continue without a Self or a Soul behind them after the non-functioning of the body?

When this physical body is no more capable of functioning, energies do not die with it, but continue to take some other shape or form, which we call another life. In a child all the physical, mental and intellectual faculties are tender and weak, but they have within them the potentiality of producing a full grown man. Physical and mental energies which constitute the so-called being have within themselves the power to take a new form, and grow gradually and gather force to the full.

[1] Prmj. I (PTS), p. 78. '*Khandhesu jāyamānesu jīyamānesu mīyamānesu ca khaṇe khaṇe tvaṃ bhikkhu jāyase ca jīyase ca mīyase ca.*' This is quoted in the *Paramatthajotikā* Commentary as the Buddha's own words. So far I have not been able to trace this passage back to its original text.

As there is no permanent, unchanging substance, nothing passes from one moment to the next. So quite obviously, nothing permanent or unchanging can pass or transmigrate from one life to the next. It is a series that continues unbroken, but changes every moment. The series is, really speaking, nothing but movement. It is like a flame that burns through the night: it is not the same flame nor is it another. A child grows up to be a man of sixty. Certainly the man of sixty is not the same as the child of sixty years ago, nor is he another person. Similarly, a person who dies here and is reborn elsewhere is neither the same person, nor another (*na ca so na ca añño*). It is the continuity of the same series. The difference between death and birth is only a thought-moment: the last thought-moment in this life conditions the first thought-moment in the so-called next life, which, in fact, is the continuity of the same series. During this life itself, too, one thought-moment conditions the next thought-moment. So from the Buddhist point of view, the question of life after death is not a great mystery, and a Buddhist is never worried about this problem.

As long as there is this 'thirst' to be and to become, the cycle of continuity (*saṃsāra*) goes on. It can stop only when its driving force, this 'thirst', is cut off through wisdom which sees Reality, Truth, Nirvāṇa.

CHAPTER IV

THE THIRD NOBLE TRUTH:

NIRODHA: 'The Cessation of *Dukkha*'

The Third Noble Truth is that there is emancipation, liberation, freedom from suffering, from the continuity of *dukkha*. This is called the Noble Truth of the Cessation of *dukkha* (*Dukkhanirodha-ariyasacca*), which is *Nibbāna*, more popularly known in its Sanskrit form of *Nirvāṇa*.

To eliminate *dukkha* completely one has to eliminate the main root of *dukkha*, which is 'thirst' (*taṇhā*), as we saw earlier. Therefore Nirvāṇa is known also by the term *Taṇhakkhaya* 'Extinction of Thirst'.

Now you will ask: But what is Nirvāṇa? Volumes have been written in reply to this quite natural and simple question; they have, more and more, only confused the issue rather than clarified it. The only reasonable reply to give to the question is that it can never be answered completely and satisfactorily in words, because human language is too poor to express the real nature of the Absolute Truth or Ultimate Reality which is Nirvāṇa. Language is created and used by masses of human beings to express things and ideas experienced by their sense organs and their mind. A supramundane experience like that of the Absolute Truth is not of such a category. Therefore there cannot be words to express that experience, just as the fish had no words in his vocabulary to express the nature of the solid land. The tortoise told his friend the fish that he (the tortoise) just returned to the lake after a walk on the land. 'Of course' the fish said, 'You mean swimming.' The tortoise tried to explain that one couldn't swim on the land, that it was solid, and that one walked on it. But the fish insisted that there could be nothing like it, that it must be liquid like his lake, with waves, and that one must be able to dive and swim there.

Words are symbols representing things and ideas known to us; and these symbols do not and cannot convey the true nature of even ordinary things. Language is considered deceptive and misleading in the matter of understanding of the Truth. So the *Laṅkāvatāra-sūtra* says that ignorant people get stuck in words like an elephant in the mud.[1]

Nevertheless we cannot do without language. But if Nirvāṇa is to be expressed and explained in positive terms, we are likely immediately to grasp an idea associated with those terms, which may be quite the contrary. Therefore it is generally expressed in negative terms[2]—a less dangerous mode perhaps. So it is often referred to by such negative terms as *Taṇhakkhaya* 'Extinction of Thirst', *Asaṃkhata* 'Uncompound', 'Unconditioned', *Virāga* 'Absence of desire', *Nirodha* 'Cessation', *Nibbāna* 'Blowing out' or 'Extinction'.

Let us consider a few definitions and descriptions of Nirvāṇa as found in the original Pali texts:

'It is the complete cessation of that very 'thirst' (*taṇhā*), giving it up, renouncing it, emancipation from it, detachment from it.'[3]

'Calming of all conditioned things, giving up of all defilments, extinction of 'thirst', detachment, cessation, Nibbāna.'[4]

'O bhikkhus, what is the Absolute (*Asaṃkhata,* Unconditioned)? It is, O bhikkhus, the extinction of desire (*rāgakkhayo*) the extinction of hatred (*dosakkhayo*), the extinction of illusion (*mohakkhayo*). This, O bhikkhus, is called the Absolute.'[5]

'O Rādha, the extinction of "thirst" (*Taṇhakkhayo*) is Nibbāna.'[6]

'O bhikkhus, whatever there may be things conditioned or unconditioned, among them detachment (*virāga*) is the highest.

[1]Lanka. p. 113.

[2]Sometimes positive terms like *Siva* 'Auspicious', 'Good', *Khema* 'Safety', *Suddhi* 'Purity', *Dīpa* 'Island', *Saraṇa* 'Refuge', *Tāṇa* 'Protection', *Pāra* 'Opposite shore', 'Other side', *Santi* 'Peace', 'Tranquility' are used to denote Nirvāṇa. There are 32 synonyms for Nibbāna in the *Asaṃkhata-saṃyutta* of the *Saṃyutta-nikāya*. They are mostly metaphorical.

[3]Mhvg. (Alutgama, 1922), p. 10; S V p. 421. It is interesting to note that this definition of *Nirodha* 'Cessation of *Dukkha*', which is found in the first sermon of the Buddha at Sarnath, does not contain the word *Nibbāna,* though the definition means it.

[4]S I, p. 136.

[5]*Ibid.* IV, p. 359.

[6]*Ibid.* III, p. 190.

That is to say, freedom from conceit, destruction of thirst,[1] the uprooting of attachment, the cutting off of continuity, the extinction of "thirst" (*taṇhā*), detachment, cessation, Nibbāna.'[2]

The reply of Sāriputta, the chief disciple of the Buddha, to a direct question 'What is Nibbāna?' posed by a Parivrājaka, is identical with the definition of *Asaṃkhata* given by the Buddha (above): 'The extinction of desire, the extinction of hatred, the extinction of illusion.'[3]

'The abandoning and destruction of desire and craving for these Five Aggregates of Attachment: that is the cessation of *dukkha*.'[4]

'The cessation of Continuity and becoming (*Bhavanirodha*) is Nibbāna.'[5]

And further, referring to Nirvāṇa the Buddha says:

'O bhikkhus, there is the unborn, ungrown, and unconditioned. Were there not the unborn, ungrown, and unconditioned, there would be no escape for the born, grown, and conditioned. Since there is the unborn, ungrown, and unconditioned, so there is escape for the born, grown, and conditioned.'[6]

'Here the four elements of solidity, fluidity, heat and motion have no place; the notions of length and breadth, the subtle and the gross, good and evil, name and form are altogether destroyed; neither this world nor the other, nor coming, going or standing, neither death nor birth, nor sense-objects are to be found.'[7]

Because Nirvāṇa is thus expressed in negative terms, there are many who have got a wrong notion that it is negative, and expresses self-annihilation. Nirvāṇa is definitely no annihilation of self, because there is no self to annihilate. If at all, it is the annihilation of the illusion, of the false idea of self.

It is incorrect to say that Nirvāṇa is negative or positive. The ideas of 'negative' and 'positive' are relative, and are within the

[1]Here the word *pipāsa* which lit. means thirst.
[2]A (PTS) II, p. 34.
[3]S (PTS) IV, p. 251.
[4]Sāriputta's words. M I, (PTS), p. 191.
[5]Words of Musīla, another disciple of the Buddha. S II (PTS), p. 117.
[6]Ud. (Colombo, 1929), p. 129.
[7]*Ibid.* p. 128; D I (Colombo, 1929), p. 172.

realm of duality. These terms cannot be applied to Nirvāṇa, Absolute Truth, which is beyond duality and relativity.

A negative word need not necessarily indicate a negative state. The Pali or Sanskrit word for health is *ārogya*, a negative term, which literally means 'absence of illness'. But *ārogya* (health) does not represent a negative state. The word 'Immortal' (or its Sanskrit equivalent *Amṛta* or Pali *Amata*), which also is a synonym for Nirvāṇa, is negative, but it does not denote a negative state. The negation of negative values is not negative. One of the well-known synonyms for Nirvāṇa is 'Freedom' (Pali *Mutti*, Skt. *Mukti*). Nobody would say that freedom is negative. But even freedom has a negative side: freedom is always a liberation from something which is obstructive, which is evil, which is negative. But freedom is not negative. So Nirvāṇa, *Mutti* or *Vimutti,* the Absolute Freedom, is freedom from all evil, freedom from craving, hatred and ignorance, freedom from all terms of duality, relativity, time and space.

We may get some idea of Nirvāṇa as Absolute Truth from the *Dhātuvibhaṅga-sutta* (No. 140) of the *Majjhima-nikāya.* This extremely important discourse was delivered by the Buddha to Pukkusāti (already mentioned), whom the Master found to be intelligent and earnest, in the quiet of the night in a potter's shed. The essence of the relevant portions of the sutta is as follows:

A man is composed of six elements: solidity, fluidity, heat, motion, space and consciousness. He analyses them and finds that none of them is 'mine', or 'me', or 'my self'. He understands how consciousness appears and disappears, how pleasant, unpleasant and neutral sensations appear and disappear. Through this knowledge his mind becomes detached. Then he finds within him a pure equanimity (*upekhā*), which he can direct towards the attainment of any high spiritual state, and he knows that thus this pure equanimity will last for a long period. But then he thinks:

'If I focus this purified and cleansed equanimity on the Sphere of Infinite Space and develop a mind conforming thereto, that is a mental creation (*saṃkhataṃ*).[1] If I focus this purified and cleansed equanimity on the Sphere of Infinite Consciousness . . . on the

[1]Notice that all the spiritual and mystic states, however pure and high they may be, are mental creations, mind-made, conditioned and compound (*saṃkhata*). They are not Reality, not Truth (*sacca*).

Sphere of Nothingness . . . or on the Sphere of Neither-perception nor Non-perception and develop a mind conforming thereto, that is a mental creation.' Then he neither mentally creates nor wills continuity and becoming (*bhava*) or annihilation (*vibhava*).[1] As he does not construct or does not will continuity and becoming or annihilation, he does not cling to anything in the world; as he does not cling, he is not anxious; as he is not anxious, he is completely calmed within (fully blown out within *paccattaṃ yeva parinibbāyati*). And he knows: 'Finished is birth, lived is pure life, what should be done is done, nothing more is left to be done.'[2]

Now, when he experiences a pleasant, unpleasant or neutral sensation, he knows that it is impermanent, that it does not bind him, that it is not experienced with passion. Whatever may be the sensation, he experiences it without being bound to it (*visaṃyutto*). He knows that all those sensations will be pacified with the dissolution of the body, just as the flame of a lamp goes out when oil and wick give out.

'Therefore, O bhikkhu, a person so endowed is endowed with the absolute wisdom, for the knowledge of the extinction of all *dukkha* is the absolute noble wisdom.

'This his deliverance, founded on Truth, is unshakable. O bhikkhu, that which is unreality (*mosadhamma*) is false; that which is reality (*amosadhamma*), Nibbāna, is Truth (*Sacca*). Therefore, O bhikkhu, a person so endowed is endowed with this Absolute Truth. For, the Absolute Noble Truth (*paramaṃ ariyasaccaṃ*) is Nibbāna, which is Reality.'

Elsewhere the Buddha unequivocally uses the word Truth in place of Nibbāna: 'I will teach you the Truth and the Path leading to the Truth.'[3] Here Truth definitely means Nirvāṇa.

Now, what is Absolute Truth? According to Buddhism, the Absolute Truth is that there is nothing absolute in the world, that everything is relative, conditioned and impermanent, and that there is no unchanging, everlasting, absolute substance like Self, Soul or *Ātman* within or without. This is the Absolute

[1]This means that he does not produce new karma, because now he is free from 'thirst', will, volition.

[2]This expression means that now he is an Arahant.

[3]S V (PTS), p. 369.

Truth. Truth is never negative, though there is a popular expression as negative truth. The realization of this Truth, i.e., to see things as they are (*yathābhūtaṃ*) without illusion or ignorance (*avijjā*),[1] is the extinction of craving 'thirst' (*Taṇhakkhaya*), and the cessation (*Nirodha*) of *dukkha*, which is Nirvāṇa. It is interesting and useful to remember here the Mahāyāna view of Nirvāṇa as not being different from *Saṃsāra*.[2] The same thing is Saṃsāra or Nirvāṇa according to the way you look at it—subjectively or objectively. This Mahāyāna view was probably developed out of the ideas found in the original Theravāda Pali texts, to which we have just referred in our brief discussion.

It is incorrect to think that Nirvāṇa is the natural result of the extinction of craving. Nirvāṇa is not the result of anything. If it would be a result, then it would be an effect produced by a cause. It would be *saṃkhata* 'produced' and 'conditioned'. Nirvāṇa is neither cause nor effect. It is beyond cause and effect. Truth is not a result nor an effect. It is not produced like a mystic, spiritual, mental state, such as *dhyāna* or *samādhi*. TRUTH IS. NIRVĀṆA IS. The only thing you can do is to see it, to realize it. There is a path leading to the realization of Nirvāṇa. But Nirvāṇa is not the result of this path.[3] You may get to the mountain along a path, but the mountain is not the result, not an effect of the path. You may see a light, but the light is not the result of your eyesight.

People often ask: What is there after Nirvāṇa? This question cannot arise, because Nirvāṇa is the Ultimate Truth. If it is Ultimate, there can be nothing after it. If there is anything after Nirvāṇa, then that will be the Ultimate Truth and not Nirvāṇa. A monk named Rādha put this question to the Buddha in a different form: 'For what purpose (or end) is Nirvāṇa?' This question presupposes something after Nirvāṇa, when it postulates some purpose or end for it. So the Buddha answered: 'O Rādha, this question could not catch its limit (i.e., it is beside the

[1]Cf. *Lanka*. p. 200; 'O Mahāmati, Nirvāṇa means to see the state of things as they are.'

[2]Nāgārjuna clearly says that '*Saṃsāra* has no difference whatever from Nirvāṇa and Nirvāṇa has no difference whatever from *Saṃsāra*.' (Madhya. Kari XXV, 19).

[3]It is useful to remember here that among nine supra-mundane *dharmas* (*navalokuttara-dhamma*) Nirvāṇa is beyond *magga* (path) and *phala* (fruition).

point). One lives the holy life with Nirvāṇa as its final plunge (into the Absolute Truth), as its goal, as its ultimate end.'[1]

Some popular inaccurately phrased expressions like 'The Buddha entered into Nirvāṇa or Parinirvāṇa after his death' have given rise to many imaginary speculations about Nirvāṇa.[2] The moment you hear the phrase that 'the Buddha entered into Nirvāṇa or Parinirvāṇa', you take Nirvāṇa to be a state, or a realm, or a position in which there is some sort of existence, and try to imagine it in terms of the senses of the word 'existence' as it is known to you. This popular expression 'entered into Nirvāṇa' has no equivalent in the orginal texts. There is no such thing as 'entering into Nirvāṇa after death'. There is a word *parinibbuto* used to denote the death of the Buddha or an Arahant who has realized Nirvāṇa, but it does not mean 'entering into Nirvāṇa'. *Parinibbuto* simply means 'fully passed away', 'fully blown out' or 'fully extinct', because the Buddha or an Arahant has no re-existence after his death.

Now another question arises: What happens to the Buddha or an Arahant after his death, *parinirvāṇa*? This comes under the category of unanswered questions (*avyākata*).[3] Even when the Buddha spoke about this, he indicated that no words in our vocabulary could express what happens to an Arahant after his death. In reply to a Parivrājaka named Vaccha, the Buddha said that terms like 'born' or 'not born' do not apply in the case of an Arahant, because those things—matter, sensation, perception, mental activities, consciousness—with which the terms like 'born' and 'not born' are associated, are completely destroyed and uprooted, never to rise again after his death.[4]

An Arahant after his death is often compared to a fire gone out when the supply of wood is over, or to the flame of a lamp gone out when the wick and oil are finished.[5] Here it should

[1]S III (PTS), p. 189.

[2]There are some who write 'after the Nirvāṇa of the Buddha' instead of 'after the Parinirvāṇa of the Buddha'. 'After the Nirvāṇa of the Buddha' has no meaning, and the expression is unknown in Buddhist literature. It is always 'after the Parinirvāṇa of the Buddha'.

[3]S IV (PTS), p. 375 f.

[4]M I (PTS), p. 486.

[5]*Ibid.* I, p. 487; III, p. 245; Sn (PTS), v. 232 (p. 41).

be clearly and distinctly understood, without any confusion, that what is compared to a flame or a fire gone out is *not* Nirvāṇa, but the 'being' composed of the Five Aggregates who realized Nirvāṇa. This point has to be emphasized because many people, even some great scholars, have misunderstood and misinterpreted this simile as referring to Nirvāṇa. Nirvāṇa is never compared to a fire or a lamp gone out.

There is another popular question: If there is no Self, no *Ātman*, who realizes Nirvāṇa? Before we go on to Nirvāṇa, let us ask the question: Who thinks now, if there is no Self? We have seen earlier that it is the thought that thinks, that there is no thinker behind the thought. In the same way, it is wisdom (*paññā*), realization, that realizes. There is no other self behind the realization. In the discussion of the origin of *dukkha* we saw that whatever it may be—whether being, or thing, or system—if it is of the nature of arising, it has within itself the nature, the germ, of its cessation, its destruction. Now *dukkha, saṃsāra*, the cycle of continuity, is of the nature of arising; it must also be of the nature of cessation. *Dukkha* arises because of 'thirst' (*taṇhā*), and it ceases because of wisdom (*paññā*). 'Thirst' and wisdom are both within the Five Aggregates, as we saw earlier.[1]

Thus, the germ of their arising as well as that of their cessation are both within the Five Aggregates. This is the real meaning of the Buddha's well-known statement: 'Within this fathom-long sentient body itself, I postulate the world, the arising of the world, the cessation of the world, and the path leading to the cessation of the world.'[2] This means that all the Four Noble Truths are found within the Five Aggregates, i.e., within ourselves. (Here the word 'world' (*loka*) is used in place of *dukkha*). This also means that there is no external power that produces the arising and the cessation of *dukkha*.

When wisdom is developed and cultivated according to the Fourth Noble Truth (the next to be taken up), it sees the secret of life, the reality of things as they are. When the secret is discovered, when the Truth is seen, all the forces which feverishly produce the continuity of *saṃsāra* in illusion become calm and incapable of

[1]See Aggregate of Formations above pp. 22, 31.

[2]A (Colombo, 1929), p. 218.

producing any more karma-formations, because there is no more illusion, no more 'thirst' for continuity. It is like a mental disease which is cured when the cause or the secret of the malady is discovered and seen by the patient.

In almost all religions the *summum bonum* can be attained only after death. But Nirvāṇa can be realized in this very life; it is not necessary to wait till you die to 'attain' it.

He who has realized the Truth, Nirvāṇa, is the happiest being in the world. He is free from all 'complexes' and obsessions, the worries and troubles that torment others. His mental health is perfect. He does not repent the past, nor does he brood over the future. He lives fully in the present.[1] Therefore he appreciates and enjoys things in the purest sense without self-projections. He is joyful, exultant, enjoying the pure life, his faculties pleased, free from anxiety, serene and peaceful.[2] As he is free from selfish desire, hatred, ignorance, conceit, pride, and all such 'defilements', he is pure and gentle, full of universal love, compassion, kindness, sympathy, understanding and tolerance. His service to others is of the purest, for he has no thought of self. He gains nothing, accumulates nothing, not even anything spiritual, because he is free from the illusion of Self, and the 'thirst' for becoming.

Nirvāṇa is beyond all terms of duality and relativity. It is therefore beyond our conceptions of good and evil, right and wrong, existence and non-existence. Even the word 'happiness' (*sukha*) which is used to describe Nirvāṇa has an entirely different sense here. Sāriputta once said: 'O friend, Nirvāṇa is happiness! Nirvāṇa is happiness!' Then Udāyi asked: 'But, friend Sāriputta, what happiness can it be if there is no sensation?' Sāriputta's reply was highly philosophical and beyond ordinary comprehension: 'That there is no sensation itself is happiness'.

Nirvāṇa is beyond logic and reasoning (*atakkāvacara*). However much we may engage, often as a vain intellectual pastime, in highly speculative discussions regarding Nirvāṇa or Ultimate Truth or Reality, we shall never understand it that way. A child in the kindergarten should not quarrel about the theory of relativity. Instead, if he follows his studies patiently and diligently,

[1] S I (PTS), p. 5.
[2] M II (PTS), p. 121.

one day he may understand it. Nirvāṇa is 'to be realized by the wise within themselves' (*paccattaṃ veditabbo viññūhi*). If we follow the Path patiently and with diligence, train and purify ourselves earnestly, and attain the necessary spiritual development, we may one day realize it within ourselves—without taxing ourselves with puzzling and high-sounding words.

Let us therefore now turn to the Path which leads to the realization of Nirvāṇa.

CHAPTER V

THE FOURTH NOBLE TRUTH:

MAGGA: 'The Path'

The Fourth Noble Truth is that of the Way leading to the Cessation of *Dukkha* (*Dukkhanirodhagāminīpaṭipadā-ariyasacca*). This is known as the 'Middle Path' (*Majjhimā Paṭipadā*), because it avoids two extremes: one extreme being the search for happiness through the pleasures of the senses, which is 'low, common, unprofitable and the way of the ordinary people'; the other being the search for happiness through self-mortification in different forms of asceticism, which is 'painful, unworthy and unprofitable'. Having himself first tried these two extremes, and having found them to be useless, the Buddha discovered through personal experience the Middle Path 'which gives vision and knowledge, which leads to Calm, Insight, Enlightenment, Nirvāṇa'. This Middle Path is generally referred to as the Noble Eightfold Path (*Ariya-Aṭṭhaṅgika-Magga*), because it is composed of eight categories or divisions: namely,

1. Right Understanding (*Sammā diṭṭhi*),
2. Right Thought (*Sammā saṅkappa*),
3. Right Speech (*Sammā vācā*),
4. Right Action (*Sammā kammanta*),
5. Right Livelihood (*Sammā ājīva*),
6. Right Effort (*Sammā vāyāma*),
7. Right Mindfulness (*Sammā sati*),
8. Right Concentration (*Sammā samādhi*).

Practically the whole teaching of the Buddha, to which he devoted himself during 45 years, deals in some way or other with this Path. He explained it in different ways and in different words to different people, according to the stage of their development and their capacity to understand and follow him. But the essence of those many thousand discourses scattered in the Buddhist Scriptures is found in the Noble Eightfold Path.

It should not be thought that the eight categories or divisions of the Path should be followed and practised one after the other in the numerical order as given in the usual list above. But they are to be developed more or less simultaneously, as far as possible according to the capacity of each individual. They are all linked together and each helps the cultivation of the others.

These eight factors aim at promoting and perfecting the three essentials of Buddhist training and discipline: namely: (*a*) Ethical Conduct (*Sīla*), (*b*) Mental Discipline (*Samādhi*) and (*c*) Wisdom (*Paññā*).[1] It will therefore be more helpful for a coherent and better understanding of the eight divisions of the Path, if we group them and explain them according to these three heads.

Ethical Conduct (*Sīla*) is built on the vast conception of universal love and compassion for all living beings, on which the Buddha's teaching is based. It is regrettable that many scholars forget this great ideal of the Buddha's teaching, and indulge in only dry philosophical and metaphysical divagations when they talk and write about Buddhism. The Buddha gave his teaching 'for the good of the many, for the happiness of the many, out of compassion for the world' (*bahujanahitāya bahujanasukhāya lokānukampāya*).

According to Buddhism for a man to be perfect there are two qualities that he should develop equally: compassion (*karuṇā*) on one side, and wisdom (*paññā*) on the other. Here compassion represents love, charity, kindness, tolerance and such noble qualities on the emotional side, or qualities of the heart, while wisdom would stand for the intellectual side or the qualities of the mind. If one develops only the emotional neglecting the intellectual, one may become a good-hearted fool; while to develop only the intellectual side neglecting the emotional may turn one into a hard-hearted intellect without feeling for others. Therefore, to be perfect one has to develop both equally. That is the aim of the Buddhist way of life: in it wisdom and compassion are inseparably linked together, as we shall see later.

Now, in Ethical Conduct (*Sīla*), based on love and compassion,

[1] M I (PTS), p. 301.

are included three factors of the Noble Eightfold Path: namely, Right Speech, Right Action and Right Livelihood. (Nos. 3, 4 and 5 in the list).

Right speech means abstention (1) from telling lies, (2) from backbiting and slander and talk that may bring about hatred, enmity, disunity and disharmony among individuals or groups of people, (3) from harsh, rude, impolite, malicious and abusive language, and (4) from idle, useless and foolish babble and gossip. When one abstains from these forms of wrong and harmful speech one naturally has to speak the truth, has to use words that are friendly and benevolent, pleasant and gentle, meaningful and useful. One should not speak carelessly: speech should be at the right time and place. If one cannot say something useful, one should keep 'noble silence'.

Right Action aims at promoting moral, honourable and peaceful conduct. It admonishes us that we should abstain from destroying life, from stealing, from dishonest dealings, from illegitimate sexual intercourse, and that we should also help others to lead a peaceful and honourable life in the right way.

Right Livelihood means that one should abstain from making one's living through a profession that brings harm to others, such as trading in arms and lethal weapons, intoxicating drinks, poisons, killing animals, cheating, etc., and should live by a profession which is honourable, blameless and innocent of harm to others. One can clearly see here that Buddhism is strongly opposed to any kind of war, when it lays down that trade in arms and lethal weapons is an evil and unjust means of livelihood.

These three factors (Right Speech, Right Action and Right Livelihood) of the Eightfold Path constitute Ethical Conduct. It should be realized that the Buddhist ethical and moral conduct aims at promoting a happy and harmonious life both for the individual and for society. This moral conduct is considered as the indispensable foundation for all higher spiritual attainments. No spiritual development is possible without this moral basis.

Next comes Mental Discipline, in which are included three other factors of the Eightfold Path: namely, Right Effort, Right Mindfulness (or Attentiveness) and Right Concentration. (Nos. 6, 7 and 8 in the list).

Right Effort is the energetic will (1) to prevent evil and unwholesome states of mind from arising, and (2) to get rid of such evil and unwholesome states that have already arisen within a man, and also (3) to produce, to cause to arise, good and wholesome states of mind not yet arisen, and (4) to develop and bring to perfection the good and wholesome states of mind already present in a man.

Right Mindfulness (or Attentiveness) is to be diligently aware, mindful and attentive with regard to (1) the activities of the body (*kāya*), (2) sensations or feelings (*vedanā*), (3) the activities of the mind (*citta*) and (4) ideas, thoughts, conceptions and things (*dhamma*).

The practice of concentration on breathing (*ānāpānasati*) is one of the well-known exercises, connected with the body, for mental development. There are several other ways of developing attentiveness in relation to the body—as modes of meditation.

With regard to sensations and feelings, one should be clearly aware of all forms of feelings and sensations, pleasant, unpleasant and neutral, of how they appear and disappear within oneself.

Concerning the activities of mind, one should be aware whether one's mind is lustful or not, given to hatred or not, deluded or not, distracted or concentrated, etc. In this way one should be aware of all movements of mind, how they arise and disappear.

As regards ideas, thoughts, conceptions and things, one should know their nature, how they appear and disappear, how they are developed, how they are suppressed, and destroyed, and so on.

These four forms of mental culture or meditation are treated in detail in the *Satipaṭṭhāna-sutta* (Setting-up of Mindfulness).[1]

The third and last factor of Mental Discipline is Right Concentration leading to the four stages of *Dhyāna,* generally called trance or *recueillement*. In the first stage of *Dhyāna,* passionate desires and certain unwholesome thoughts like sensuous lust, ill-will, languor, worry, restlessness, and sceptical doubt are discarded, and feelings of joy and happiness are maintained, along with certain mental activities. In the second stage, all intellectual activities are suppressed, tranquility and 'one-pointedness' of mind developed, and the feelings of joy and happiness are still

[1]See Chapter VII on Meditation.

VII. The Buddha—from Tibet

VIII. The head of the Buddha—from Afghanistan

IX. The Buddha—from Cambodia

X. *Saṃsāra-cakra*—the Cycle of Existence and Continuity—from Tibet

retained. In the third stage, the feeling of joy, which is an active sensation, also disappears, while the disposition of happiness still remains in addition to mindful equanimity. In the fourth stage of *Dhyāna*, all sensations, even of happiness and unhappiness, of joy and sorrow, disappear, only pure equanimity and awareness remaining.

Thus the mind is trained and disciplined and developed through Right Effort, Right Mindfulness, and Right Concentration.

The remaining two factors, namely Right Thought and Right Understanding go to constitute Wisdom.

Right Thought denotes the thoughts of selfless renunciation or detachment, thoughts of love and thoughts of non-violence, which are extended to all beings. It is very interesting and important to note here that thoughts of selfless detachment, love and non-violence are grouped on the side of wisdom. This clearly shows that true wisdom is endowed with these noble qualities, and that all thoughts of selfish desire, ill-will, hatred and violence are the result of a lack of wisdom—in all spheres of life whether individual, social, or political.

Right Understanding is the understanding of things as they are, and it is the Four Noble Truths that explain things as they really are. Right Understanding therefore is ultimately reduced to the understanding of the Four Noble Truths. This understanding is the highest wisdom which sees the Ultimate Reality. According to Buddhism there are two sorts of understanding: What we generally call understanding is knowledge, an accumulated memory, an intellectual grasping of a subject according to certain given data. This is called 'knowing accordingly' (*anubodha*). It is not very deep. Real deep understanding is called 'penetration' (*paṭivedha*), seeing a thing in its true nature, without name and label. This penetration is possible only when the mind is free from all impurities and is fully developed through meditation.[1]

From this brief account of the Path, one may see that it is a way of life to be followed, practised and developed by each individual. It is self-discipline in body, word and mind, self-development and self-purification. It has nothing to do with belief, prayer, worship or ceremony. In that sense, it has nothing

[1]Vism. (PTS), p. 510.

which may popularly be called 'religious'. It is a Path leading to the realization of Ultimate Reality, to complete freedom, happiness and peace through moral, spiritual and intellectual perfection.

In Buddhist countries there are simple and beautiful customs and ceremonies on religious occasions. They have little to do with the real Path. But they have their value in satisfying certain religious emotions and the needs of those who are less advanced, and helping them gradually along the Path.

With regard to the Four Noble Truths we have four functions to perform:

The First Noble Truth is *Dukkha*, the nature of life, its suffering, its sorrows and joys, its imperfection and unsatisfactoriness, its impermanence and insubstantiality. With regard to this, our function is to understand it as a fact, clearly and completely (*pariññeyya*).

The Second Noble Truth is the Origin of *Dukkha*, which is desire, 'thirst', accompanied by all other passions, defilements and impurities. A mere understanding of this fact is not sufficient. Here our function is to discard it, to eliminate, to destroy and eradicate it (*pahātabba*).

The Third Noble Truth is the Cessation of *Dukkha*, Nirvāṇa, the Absolute Truth, the Ultimate Reality. Here our function is to realize it (*sacchikātabba*).

The Fourth Noble Truth is the Path leading to the realization of Nirvāṇa. A mere knowledge of the Path, however complete, will not do. In this case, our function is to follow it and keep to it (*bhāvetabba*).[1]

[1] Mhvg. (Alutgama, 1922), p. 10.

CHAPTER VI

THE DOCTRINE OF NO-SOUL: *ANATTA*

What in general is suggested by Soul, Self, Ego, or to use the Sanskrit expression *Ātman,* is that in man there is a permanent, everlasting and absolute entity, which is the unchanging substance behind the changing phenomenal world. According to some religions, each individual has such a separate soul which is created by God, and which, finally after death, lives eternally either in hell or heaven, its destiny depending on the judgment of its creator. According to others, it goes through many lives till it is completely purified and becomes finally united with God or Brahman, Universal Soul or *Ātman*, from which it originally emanated. This soul or self in man is the thinker of thoughts, feeler of sensations, and receiver of rewards and punishments for all its actions good and bad. Such a conception is called the idea of self.

Buddhism stands unique in the history of human thought in denying the existence of such a Soul, Self, or *Ātman*. According to the teaching of the Buddha, the idea of self is an imaginary, false belief which has no corresponding reality, and it produces harmful thoughts of 'me' and 'mine', selfish desire, craving, attachment, hatred, ill-will, conceit, pride, egoism, and other defilements, impurities and problems. It is the source of all the troubles in the world from personal conflicts to wars between nations. In short, to this false view can be traced all the evil in the world.

Two ideas are psychologically deep-rooted in man: self-protection and self-preservation. For self-protection man has created God, on whom he depends for his own protection, safety and security, just as a child depends on its parent. For self-preservation man has conceived the idea of an immortal Soul or *Ātman*, which will live eternally. In his ignorance, weakness, fear, and desire, man needs these two things to console himself. Hence he clings to them deeply and fanatically.

The Buddha's teaching does not support this ignorance, weakness, fear, and desire, but aims at making man enlightened by removing and destroying them, striking at their very root. According to Buddhism, our ideas of God and Soul are false and empty. Though highly developed as theories, they are all the same extremely subtle mental projections, garbed in an intricate metaphysical and philosophical phraseology. These ideas are so deep-rooted in man, and so near and dear to him, that he does not wish to hear, nor does he want to understand, any teaching against them.

The Buddha knew this quite well. In fact, he said that his teaching was 'against the current' (*paṭisotagāmi*), against man's selfish desires. Just four weeks after his Enlightenment, seated under a banyan tree, he thought to himself: 'I have realized this Truth which is deep, difficult to see, difficult to understand . . . comprehensible only by the wise . . . Men who are overpowered by passions and surrounded by a mass of darkness cannot see this Truth, which is against the current, which is lofty, deep, subtle and hard to comprehend.'

With these thoughts in his mind, the Buddha hesitated for a moment, whether it would not be in vain if he tried to explain to the world the Truth he had just realized. Then he compared the world to a lotus pond: In a lotus pond there are some lotuses still under water; there are others which have risen only up to the water level; there are still others which stand above water and are untouched by it. In the same way in this world, there are men at different levels of development. Some would understand the Truth. So the Buddha decided to teach it.[1]

The doctrine of *Anatta* or No-Soul is the natural result of, or the corollary to, the analysis of the Five Aggregates and the teaching of Conditioned Genesis (*Paṭicca-samuppāda*).[2]

We have seen earlier, in the discussion of the First Noble Truth (*Dukkha*), that what we call a being or an individual is composed of the Five Aggregates, and that when these are analysed and examined, there is nothing behind them which can be taken as 'I', *Ātman*, or Self, or any unchanging abiding substance. That is the analytical method. The same result is arrived at through the

[1]Mhvg. (Alutgama, 1922), p. 4 f; M I (PTS), p. 167 f.

[2]Explained below.

doctrine of Conditioned Genesis which is the synthetical method, and according to this nothing in the world is absolute. Everything is conditioned, relative, and interdependent. This is the Buddhist theory of relativity.

Before we go into the question of *Anatta* proper, it is useful to have a brief idea of the Conditioned Genesis. The principle of this doctrine is given in a short formula of four lines:

When this is, that is (*Imasmiṃ sati idaṃ hoti*);
This arising, that arises (*Imassuppādā idaṃ uppajjati*);
When this is not, that is not (*Imasmiṃ asati idaṃ na hoti*);
This ceasing, that ceases (*Imassa nirodhā idaṃ nirujjhati*).[1]

On this principle of conditionality, relativity and interdependence, the whole existence and continuity of life and its cessation are explained in a detailed formula which is called *Paṭicca-samuppāda* 'Conditioned Genesis', consisting of twelve factors:

1. Through ignorance are conditioned volitional actions or karma-formations (*Avijjāpaccayā saṃkhārā*).
2. Through volitional actions is conditioned consciousness (*Saṃkhārapaccayā viññāṇaṃ*).
3. Through consciousness are conditioned mental and physical phenomena (*Viññāṇapaccayā nāmarūpaṃ*).
4. Through mental and physical phenomena are conditioned the six faculties (i.e., five physical sense-organs and mind) (*Nāmarūpapaccayā saḷāyatanaṃ*).
5. Through the six faculties is conditioned (sensorial and mental) contact (*Saḷāyatanapaccayā phasso*).
6. Through (sensorial and mental) contact is conditioned sensation (*Phassapaccayā vedanā*).
7. Through sensation is conditioned desire, 'thirst' (*Vedanāpaccayā taṇhā*).
8. Through desire ('thirst') is conditioned clinging (*Taṇhāpaccayā upādānaṃ*).

[1]M III (PTS), p. 63; S II (PTS), pp. 28, 95, etc. To put it into a modern form:
When A is, B is;
A arising, B arises;
When A is not, B is not;
A ceasing, B ceases.

9. Through clinging is conditioned the process of becoming (*Upādānapaccayā bhavo*).
10. Through the process of becoming is conditioned birth (*Bhavapaccayā jāti*).
11. Through birth are conditioned (12) decay, death, lamentation, pain, etc. (*Jātipaccayā jarāmaraṇaṃ . . .*).

This is how life arises, exists and continues. If we take this formula in its reverse order, we come to the cessation of the process:

Through the complete cessation of ignorance, volitional activities or karma-formations cease; through the cessation of volitional activities, consciousness ceases; . . . through the cessation of birth, decay, death, sorrow, etc., cease.

It should be clearly remembered that each of these factors is conditioned (*paṭiccasamuppanna*) as well as conditioning (*paṭicca samuppāda*).[1] Therefore they are all relative, interdependent and interconnected, and nothing is absolute or independent; hence no first cause is accepted by Buddhism as we have seen earlier.[2] Conditioned Genesis should be considered as a circle, and not as a chain.[3]

The question of Free Will has occupied an important place in Western thought and philosophy. But according to Conditioned Genesis, this question does not and cannot arise in Buddhist philosophy. If the whole of existence is relative, conditioned and interdependent, how can will alone be free? Will, like any other thought, is conditioned. So-called 'freedom' itself is conditioned and relative. There can be nothing absolutely free, physical or mental, as everything is interdependent and relative. Free Will implies a will independent of conditions, independent of cause and effect. How can a will, or anything for that matter, arise without conditions, away from cause and effect, when the whole of existence is conditioned and relative, and is within the law of cause and effect? Here again, the idea of Free Will is basically connected with the ideas of God, Soul, justice, reward and punishment. Not

[1]Vism. (PTS), p. 517.

[2]See above p. 29.

[3]Limited space does not permit a discussion here of this most important doctrine. A critical and comparative study of this subject in detail will be found in a forthcoming work on Buddhist philosophy by the present writer.

only is so-called free will not free, but even the very idea of Free Will is not free from conditions.

According to the doctrine of Conditioned Genesis, as well as according to the analysis of being into Five Aggregates, the idea of an abiding, immortal substance in man or outside, whether it is called *Ātman*, 'I', Soul, Self, or Ego, is considered only a false belief, a mental projection. This is the Buddhist doctrine of *Anatta,* No-Soul or No-Self.

In order to avoid a confusion it should be mentioned here that there are two kinds of truths: conventional truth (*sammuti-sacca,* Skt. *saṃvṛti-satya*) and ultimate truth (*paramattha-sacca,* Skt. *paramārtha-satya*).[1] When we use such expressions in our daily life as 'I', 'you', 'being', 'individual', etc., we do not lie because there is no self or being as such, but we speak a truth conforming to the convention of the world. But the ultimate truth is that there is no 'I' or 'being' in reality. As the *Mahāyāna-sūtrālaṅkāra* says: 'A person (*pudgala*) should be mentioned as existing only in designation (*prajñapti*) (i.e., conventionally there is a being), but not in reality (or substance *dravya*)'.[2]

'The negation of an imperishable *Ātman* is the common characteristic of all dogmatic systems of the Lesser as well as the Great Vehicle, and, there is, therefore, no reason to assume that Buddhist tradition which is in complete agreement on this point has deviated from the Buddha's original teaching.'[3]

It is therefore curious that recently there should have been a vain attempt by a few scholars[4] to smuggle the idea of self into the teaching of the Buddha, quite contrary to the spirit of Buddhism. These scholars respect, admire, and venerate the Buddha and his teaching. They look up to Buddhism. But they cannot imagine that the Buddha, whom they consider the most clear and profound thinker, could have denied the existence of an *Ātman* or Self which they need so much. They unconsciously seek the support of the Buddha for this need for eternal existence—of course not in a

[1]Sāratthа II (PTS), p. 77.

[2]Mh. sūtrālaṅkāra, XVIII 92.

[3]H. von Glasenapp, in an article 'Vedanta and Buddhism' on the question of Anatta, *The Middle Way*, February, 1957, p. 154.

[4]The late Mrs. Rhys Davids and others. See Mrs. Rhys Davids' *Gotama the Man, Sākya or Buddhist Origins, A Manual of Buddhism, What was the Original Buddhism,* etc.

petty individual self with small s, but in the big Self with a capital S.

It is better to say frankly that one believes in an *Ātman* or Self. Or one may even say that the Buddha was totally wrong in denying the existence of an *Ātman*. But certainly it will not do for any one to try to introduce into Buddhism an idea which the Buddha never accepted, as far as we can see from the extant original texts.

Religions which believe in God and Soul make no secret of these two ideas; on the contrary, they proclaim them, constantly and repeatedly, in the most eloquent terms. If the Buddha had accepted these two ideas, so important in all religions, he certainly would have declared them publicly, as he had spoken about other things, and would not have left them hidden to be discovered only 25 centuries after his death.

People become nervous at the idea that through the Buddha's teaching of *Anatta*, the self they imagine they have is going to be destroyed. The Buddha was not unaware of this.

A bhikkhu once asked him: 'Sir, is there a case where one is tormented when something permanent within oneself is not found?'

'Yes, bhikkhu, there is,' answered the Buddha. 'A man has the following view: "The universe is that *Ātman*, I shall be that after death, permanent, abiding, ever-lasting, unchanging, and I shall exist as such for eternity". He hears the Tathāgata or a disciple of his, preaching the doctrine aiming at the complete destruction of all speculative views . . . aiming at the extinction of "thirst", aiming at detachment, cessation, Nirvāṇa. Then that man thinks: "I will be annihilated, I will be destroyed, I will be no more." So he mourns, worries himself, laments, weeps, beating his breast, and becomes bewildered. Thus, O bhikkhu, there is a case where one is tormented when something permanent within oneself is not found.'[1]

Elsewhere the Buddha says: 'O bhikkhus, this idea that I may not be, I may not have, is frightening to the uninstructed worldling.'[2]

Those who want to find a 'Self' in Buddhism argue as follows: It is true that the Buddha analyses being into matter, sensation,

[1]M I (PTS), pp. 136-137.
[2]Quoted in MA II (PTS), p. 112.

perception, mental formations, and consciousness, and says that none of these things is self. But he does not say that there is no self at all in man or anywhere else, apart from these aggregates.

This position is untenable for two reasons:

One is that, according to the Buddha's teaching, a being is composed only of these Five Aggregates, and nothing more. Nowhere has he said that there was anything more than these Five Aggregates in a being.

The second reason is that the Buddha denied categorically, in unequivocal terms, in more than one place, the existence of *Ātman*, Soul, Self, or Ego within man or without, or anywhere else in the universe. Let us take some examples.

In the *Dhammapada* there are three verses extremely important and essential in the Buddha's teaching. They are nos. 5, 6 and 7 of chapter XX (or verses 277, 278, 279).

The first two verses say:

'All conditioned things are impermanent' (*Sabbe SAṂKHĀRĀ aniccā*), and 'All conditioned things are *dukkha*' (*Sabbe SAṂKHĀRĀ dukkhā*).

The third verse says:

'All *dhammas* are without self' (*Sabbe DHAMMĀ anattā*).[1]

Here it should be carefully observed that in the first two verses the word *saṃkhārā* 'conditioned things' is used. But in its place in the third verse the word *dhammā* is used. Why didn't the third verse use the word *saṃkhārā* 'conditioned things' as the previous two verses, and why did it use the term *dhammā* instead? Here lies the crux of the whole matter.

The term *saṃkhāra*[2] denotes the Five Aggregates, all conditioned, interdependent, relative things and states, both physical and mental. If the third verse said: 'All *saṃkhārā* (conditioned things) are without self', then one might think that, although conditioned things are without self, yet there may be a Self outside conditioned things, outside the Five Aggregates. It is in

[1] F. L. Woodward's translation of the word *dhammā* here by 'All states compounded' is quite wrong. (The Buddha's *Path of Virtue*, Adyar, Madras, India, 1929, p. 69.) 'All states compounded' means only *saṃkhārā*, but not *dhammā*.

[2] *Saṃkhāra* in the list of the Five Aggregates means 'Mental Formations' or 'Mental Activities' producing karmic effects. But here it means all conditioned or compounded things, including all the Five Aggregates. The term *saṃkhāra* has different connotations in different contexts.

order to avoid misunderstanding that the term *dhammā* is used in the third verse.

The term *dhamma* is much wider than *saṃkhāra*. There is no term in Buddhist terminology wider than *dhamma*. It includes not only the conditioned things and states, but also the non-conditioned, the Absolute, Nirvāṇa. There is nothing in the universe or outside, good or bad, conditioned or non-conditioned, relative or absolute, which is not included in this term. Therefore, it is quite clear that, according to this statement: 'All *dhammas* are without Self', there is no Self, no *Ātman*, not only in the Five Aggregates, but nowhere else too outside them or apart from them.[1]

This means, according to the Theravāda teaching, that there is no self either in the individual (*puggala*) or in *dhammas*. The Mahāyāna Buddhist philosophy maintains exactly the same position, without the slightest difference, on this point, putting emphasis on *dharma-nairātmya* as well as on *pudgala-nairātmya*.

In the *Alagaddūpama-sutta* of the *Majjhima-nikāya*, addressing his disciples, the Buddha said : 'O bhikkhus, accept a soul-theory (*Attavāda*) in the acceptance of which there would not arise grief, lamentation, suffering, distress and tribulation. But, do you see, O bhikkhus, such a soul-theory in the acceptance of which there would not arise grief, lamentation, suffering, distress and tribulation?'

'Certainly not, Sir.'

'Good, O bhikkhus. I, too, O bhikkhus, do not see a soul-theory, in the acceptance of which there would not arise grief, lamentation, suffering, distress and tribulation.'[2]

If there had been any soul-theory which the Buddha had accepted, he would certainly have explained it here, because he asked the bhikkhus to accept that soul-theory which did not produce suffering. But in the Buddha's view, there is no such soul-theory, and any soul-theory, whatever it may be, however subtle and sublime, is false and imaginary, creating all kinds of problems, producing in its train grief, lamentation, suffering, distress, tribulation and trouble.

[1]Cf. also *Sabbe saṃkhārā aniccā* 'All conditioned things are impermanent', *Sabbe dhammā anattā* 'All *dhammas* are without self'. M I (PTS), p. 228; S II pp. 132, 133.

[2]M I (PTS), p. 137.

Continuing the discourse the Buddha said in the same *sutta*: 'O bhikkhus, when neither self nor anything pertaining to self can truly and really be found, this speculative view: "The universe is that *Ātman* (Soul); I shall be that after death, permanent, abiding, ever-lasting, unchanging, and I shall exist as such for eternity"—is it not wholly and completely foolish?'[1]

Here the Buddha explicitly states that an *Ātman*, or Soul, or Self, is nowhere to be found in reality, and it is foolish to believe that there is such a thing.

Those who seek a self in the Buddha's teaching quote a few examples which they first translate wrongly, and then misinterpret. One of them is the well-known line *Attā hi attano nātho* from the *Dhammapada* (XII, 4, or verse 160), which is translated as 'Self is the lord of self', and then interpreted to mean that the big Self is the lord of the small self.

First of all, this translation is incorrect. *Attā* here does not mean self in the sense of soul. In Pali the word *attā* is generally used as a reflexive or indefinite pronoun, except in a few cases where it specifically and philosophically refers to the soul-theory, as we have seen above. But in general usage, as in the XII chapter in the *Dhammapada* where this line occurs, and in many other places, it is used as a reflexive or indefinite pronoun meaning 'myself', 'yourself', 'himself', 'one', 'oneself', etc.[2]

Next, the word *nātho* does not mean 'lord', but 'refuge', 'support', 'help', 'protection'.[3] Therefore, *Attā hi attano nātho*

[1]*Ibid.*, p. 138. Referring to this passage, S. Radhakrishnan, (*Indian Philosophy*, Vol. I, London, 1940, p. 485), says: 'It is the false view that clamours for the perpetual continuance of the small self that Buddha refutes'. We cannot agree with this remark. On the contrary, the Buddha, in fact, refutes here the Universal *Ātman* or Soul. As we saw just now, in the earlier passage, the Buddha did not accept any self, great or small. In his view, all theories of *Ātman* were false, mental projections.

[2]In his article 'Vedanta and Buddhism' (The Middle Way, February, 1957), H. von Glasenapp explains this point clearly.

[3]The commentary on the Dhp. says: *Nātho'ti patiṭṭhā* '*Nātho* means support, (refuge, help, protection),' (Dhp. A III (PTS), p. 148.) The old Sinhalese *Sannaya* of the Dhp. paraphrases the word *nātho* as *pihiṭa vanneya* 'is a support (refuge, help)'. (*Dhammapada Purāṇasannaya*, Colombo, 1926, p. 77). If we take the negative form of *nātho*, this meaning becomes further confirmed: *Anātha* does not mean 'without a lord' or 'lordless', but it means 'helpless', 'supportless', 'unprotected', 'poor'. Even the PTS Pali Dictionary explains the word *nātha* as 'protector', 'refuge', 'help', but not as 'lord'. The translation of the word *Lokanātha* (s.v.) by 'Saviour of the world', just using a popular Christian expression, is not quite correct, because the Buddha is not a saviour. This epithet really means 'Refuge of the World'.

really means 'One is one's own refuge' or 'One is one's own help' or 'support'. It has nothing to do with any metaphysical soul or self. It simply means that you have to rely on yourself, and not on others.

Another example of the attempt to introduce the idea of self into the Buddha's teaching is in the well-known words *Attadīpā viharatha, attasaraṇā anaññasaraṇā*, which are taken out of context in the *Mahāparinibbāna-sutta*.[1] This phrase literally means: 'Dwell making yourselves your island (support), making yourselves your refuge, and not anyone else as your refuge.'[2] Those who wish to see a self in Buddhism interpret the words *attadīpā* and *attasaraṇā* 'taking self as a lamp', 'taking self as a refuge'.[3]

We cannot understand the full meaning and significance of the advice of the Buddha to Ānanda, unless we take into consideration the background and the context in which these words were spoken.

The Buddha was at the time staying at a village called Beluva. It was just three months before his death, *Parinirvāṇa*. At this time he was eighty years old, and was suffering from a very serious illness, almost dying (*māraṇantika*). But he thought it was not proper for him to die without breaking it to his disciples who were near and dear to him. So with courage and determination he bore all his pains, got the better of his illness, and recovered. But his health was still poor. After his recovery, he was seated one day in the shade outside his residence. Ānanda, the most devoted attendant of the Buddha, went to his beloved Master, sat near him, and said: 'Sir, I have looked after the health of the Blessed One, I have looked after him in his illness. But at the sight of the illness of the Blessed One the horizon became dim to me, and my faculties were no longer clear. Yet there was one little consolation:

[1]D II (Colombo, 1929), p. 62.

[2]Rhys Davids (*Dīgha-nikāya* Translation II, p. 108) 'Be ye lamps unto yourselves. Be ye a refuge to yourselves. Betake yourselves to no external refuge.'

[3]*Dīpa* here does not mean lamp, but it definitely means 'island'. The *Dīgha-nikāya* Commentary (DA Colombo ed. p. 380), commenting on the word *dīpa* here says: *Mahāsamuddagataṃ dīpaṃ viya attānaṃ dīpaṃ patiṭṭhaṃ katvā viharatha*. 'Dwell making yourselves an island, a support (resting place) even as an island in the great ocean.' *Saṃsāra*, the continuity of existence, is usually compared to an ocean, *saṃsāra-sāgara*, and what is required in the ocean for safety is an island, a solid land, and not a lamp.

I thought that the Blessed One would not pass away until he had left instructions touching the Order of the Sangha.'

Then the Buddha, full of compassion and human feeling, gently spoke to his devoted and beloved attendant: 'Ānanda, what does the Order of the Sangha expect from me? I have taught the *Dhamma* (Truth) without making any distinction as exoteric and esoteric. With regard to the truth, the Tathāgata has nothing like the closed fist of a teacher (*ācariya-muṭṭhi*). Surely, Ānanda, if there is anyone who thinks that he will lead the Sangha, and that the Sangha should depend on him, let him set down his instructions. But the Tathāgata has no such idea. Why should he then leave instructions concerning the Sangha? I am now old, Ānanda, eighty years old. As a worn-out cart has to be kept going by repairs, so, it seems to me, the body of the Tathāgata can only be kept going by repairs. *Therefore, Ānanda, dwell making yourselves your island (support), making yourselves, not anyone else, your refuge; making the Dhamma your island (support), the Dhamma your refuge, nothing else your refuge.*'[1]

What the Buddha wanted to convey to Ānanda is quite clear. The latter was sad and depressed. He thought that they would all be lonely, helpless, without a refuge, without a leader after their great Teacher's death. So the Buddha gave him consolation, courage, and confidence, saying that they should depend on themselves, and on the *Dhamma* he taught, and not on anyone else, or on anything else. Here the question of a metaphysical *Ātman*, or Self, is quite beside the point.

Further, the Buddha explained to Ānanda how one could be one's own island or refuge, how one could make the *Dhamma* one's own island or refuge: through the cultivation of mindfulness or awareness of the body, sensations, mind and mind-objects (the four *Satipaṭṭhānas*).[2] There is no talk at all here about an *Ātman* or Self.

Another reference, oft-quoted, is used by those who try to find *Ātman* in the Buddha's teaching. The Buddha was once seated under a tree in a forest on the way to Uruvelā from Benares. On that day, thirty friends, all of them young princes,

[1] D II (Colombo, 1929), pp. 61-62. Only the last sentence is literally translated. The rest of the story is given briefly acording to the *Mahāparinibbāna-sutta*.

[2] *Ibid.*, p. 62. For *Satipaṭṭhāna* see Chapter VII on Meditation.

went out on a picnic with their young wives into the same forest. One of the princes who was unmarried brought a prostitute with him. While the others were amusing themselves, she purloined some objects of value and disappeared. In their search for her in the forest, they saw the Buddha seated under a tree and asked him whether he had seen a woman. He enquired what was the matter. When they explained, the Buddha asked them: 'What do you think, young men? Which is better for you? To search after a woman, or to search after yourselves?'[1]

Here again it is a simple and natural question, and there is no justification for introducing far-fetched ideas of a metaphysical *Ātman* or Self into the business. They answered that it was better for them to search after themselves. The Buddha then asked them to sit down and explained the *Dhamma* to them. In the available account, in the original text of what he preached to them, not a word is mentioned about an *Ātman*.

Much has been written on the subject of the Buddha's silence when a certain Parivrājakā (Wanderer) named Vacchagotta asked him whether there was an *Ātman* or not. The story is as follows:

Vacchagotta comes to the Buddha and asks:

'Venerable Gotama, is there an *Ātman*?'

The Buddha is silent.

'Then Venerable Gotama, is there no *Ātman*?'

Again the Buddha is silent.

Vacchagotta gets up and goes away.

After the Parivrājakā had left, Ānanda asks the Buddha why he did not answer Vacchagotta's question. The Buddha explains his position:

'Ānanda, when asked by Vacchagotta the Wanderer: "Is there a self?", if I had answered: "There is a self", then, Ānanda, that would be siding with those recluses and brāhmaṇas who hold the eternalist theory (*sassata-vāda*).

'And, Ānanda, when asked by the Wanderer: "Is there no self?' if I had answered: "There is no self", then that would be siding with those recluses and brāhmaṇas who hold the annihilationist theory (*uccheda-vāda*).[2]

[1]Mhvg., (Alutgama, 1929), pp. 21-22.

[2]On another occasion the Buddha had told this same Vacchagotta that the Tathāgata had no theories, because he had seen the nature of things. (M I (PTS), p. 486.) Here too he does not want to associate himself with any theorists.

'Again, Ānanda, when asked by Vacchagotta: "Is there a self?", if I had answered: "There is a self", would that be in accordance with my knowledge that all *dhammas* are without self?'[1]

'Surely not, Sir.'

'And again, Ānanda, when asked by the Wanderer: "Is there no self?", if I had answered: "There is no self", then that would have been a greater confusion to the already confused Vacchagotta.[2] For he would have thought: Formerly indeed I had an *Ātman* (self), but now I haven't got one.'[3]

It should now be quite clear why the Buddha was silent. But it will be still clearer if we take into consideration the whole background, and the way the Buddha treated questions and questioners—which is altogether ignored by those who have discussed this problem.

The Buddha was not a computing machine giving answers to whatever questions were put to him by anyone at all, without any consideration. He was a practical teacher, full of compassion and wisdom. He did not answer questions to show his knowledge and intelligence, but to help the questioner on the way to realization. He always spoke to people bearing in mind their standard of development, their tendencies, their mental make-up, their character, their capacity to understand a particular question.[4]

[1]*Sabbe dhammā anattā.* (Exactly the same words as in the first line of Dhp. XX, 7 which we discussed above.) Woodward's translation of these words by 'all things are impermanent' (*Kindred Sayings* IV, p. 282) is completely wrong, probably due to an oversight. But this is a very serious mistake. This, perhaps, is one of the reasons for so much unnecessary talk on the Buddha's silence. The most important word in this context, *anatta* 'without a self', has been translated as 'impermanent'. The English translations of Pali texts contain major and minor errors of this kind—some due to carelessness or oversight, some to lack of proficiency in the original language. Whatever the cause may be, it is useful to mention here, with the deference due to those great pioneers in this field, that these errors have been responsible for a number of wrong ideas about Buddhism among people who have no access to the original texts. It is good to know therefore that Miss I. B. Horner, the Secretary of the Pali Text Society, plans to bring out revised and new translations.

[2]In fact on another occasion, evidently earlier, when the Buddha had explained a certain deep and subtle question—the question as to what happened to an Arahant after death—Vacchagotta said: 'Venerable Gotama, here I fall into ignorance, I get into confusion. Whatever little faith I had at the beginning of this conversation with the Venerable Gotama, that too is gone now.' (M I (PTS), p. 487). So the Buddha did not want to confuse him again.

[3]S IV (PTS), pp. 400-401.

[4]This knowledge of the Buddha is called *Indriyaparopariyattañāṇa*. M I (PTS), p. 70; Vibh. (PTS), p 340.

According to the Buddha, there are four ways of treating questions: (1) Some should be answered directly; (2) others should be answered by way of analysing them; (3) yet others should be answered by counter-questions; (4) and lastly, there are questions which should be put aside.[1]

There may be several ways of putting aside a question. One is to say that a particular question is not answered or explained, as the Buddha had told this very same Vacchagotta on more than one occasion, when those famous questions whether the universe is eternal or not, etc., were put to him.[2] In the same way he had replied to Māluṅkyaputta and others. But he could not say the same thing with regard to the question whether there is an *Ātman* (Self) or not, because he had always discussed and explained it. He could not say 'there is self', because it is contrary to his knowledge that 'all *dhammas* are without self'. Then he did not want to say 'there is no self', because that would unnecessarily, without any purpose, have confused and disturbed poor Vacchagotta who was already confused on a similar question, as he had himself admitted earlier.[3] He was not yet in a position to understand the idea of *Anatta*. Therefore, to put aside this question by silence was the wisest thing in this particular case.

We must not forget too that the Buddha had known Vacchagotta quite well for a long time. This was not the first occasion on which this inquiring Wanderer had come to see him. The wise and compassionate Teacher gave much thought and showed great consideration for this confused seeker. There are many references in the Pali texts to this same Vacchagotta the Wanderer, his going round quite often to see the Buddha and his disciples and putting the same kind of question again and again, evidently very much worried, almost obsessed by these problems.[4] The Buddha's silence seems to have had much more effect on Vacchagotta than any eloquent answer or discussion.[5]

[1]A (Colombo, 1929), p. 216.

[2]*E.g.* S IV (PTS), pp. 393, 395; M I (PTS), p. 484.

[3]See p. 63 n. 2.

[4]*E.g.* see S III (PTS), pp. 257-263; IV pp. 391 f., 395 f., 398 f., 400; M I, pp. 481 f., 483 f., 489 f., A V p. 193.

[5]For, we see that after some time Vacchagotta came again to see the Buddha, but this time did not ask any questions as usual, but said: "It is long since I had a talk with

XI. Sujātā offering milk-rice to the Buddha—from Borobudur, Java

XII. The head of the Buddha—from Borobudur, Java

XIII. The Buddha—from Borobudur, Java

XIV. The *Parinirvāṇa* of the Buddha—from Ajanta, India

Some people take 'self' to mean what is generally known as 'mind' or 'consciousness'. But the Buddha says that it is better for a man to take his physical body as self rather than mind, thought, or consciousness, because the former seems to be more solid than the latter, because mind, thought, or consciousness (*citta, mano, viññāṇa*) changes constantly day and night even faster than the body (*kāya*).[1]

It is the vague feeling 'I AM' that creates the idea of self which has no corresponding reality, and to see this truth is to realize Nirvāṇa, which is not very easy. In the *Saṃyutta-nikāya*[2] there is an enlightening conversation on this point between a bhikkhu named Khemaka and a group of bhikkhus.

These bhikkhus ask Khemaka whether he sees in the Five Aggregates any self or anything pertaining to a self. Khemaka replies 'No'. Then the bhikkhus say that, if so, he should be an Arahant free from all impurities. But Khemaka confesses that though he does not find in the Five Aggregates a self, or anything pertaining to a self, 'I am not an Arahant free from all impurities. O friends, with regard to the Five Aggregates of Attachment, I have a feeling "I AM", but I do not clearly see "This is I AM".' Then Khemaka explains that what he calls 'I AM' is neither matter, sensation, perception, mental formations, nor consciousness, nor anything without them. But he has the feeling 'I AM' with regard to the Five Aggregates, though he could not see clearly 'This is I AM'.[3]

He says it is like the smell of a flower: it is neither the smell of the petals, nor of the colour, nor of the pollen, but the smell of the flower.

the Venerable Gotama. It would be good if the Venerable Gotama would preach to me on good and bad (*kusalākusalaṃ*) in brief." The Buddha said that he would explain to him good and bad, in brief as well as in detail; and so he did. Ultimately Vacchagotta became a disciple of the Buddha, and following his teaching attained Arahantship, realized Truth, Nirvāṇa, and the problems of *Ātman* and other questions obsessed him no more. (M I (PTS), pp. 489 ff.)

[1]S II (PTS), p. 94. Some people think that *Ālayavijñāna* 'Store-Consciousness' (*Tathāgatagarbha*) of Mahāyāna Buddhism is something like a self. But the *Laṅkāvatāra-sūtra* categorically says that it is not *Ātman* (Lanka. p. 78-79.)

[2]S III (PTS), pp. 126 ff.

[3]This is what most people say about self even today.

Khemaka further explains that even a person who has attained the early stages of realization still retains this feeling 'I AM'. But later on, when he progresses further, this feeling of 'I AM' altogether disappears, just as the chemical smell of a freshly washed cloth disappears after a time when it is kept in a box.

This discussion was so useful and enlightening to them that at the end of it, the text says, all of them, including Khemaka himself, became Arahants free from all impurities, thus finally getting rid of 'I AM'.

According to the Buddha's teaching, it is as wrong to hold the opinion 'I have no self' (which is the annihilationist theory) as to hold the opinion 'I have self' (which is the eternalist theory), because both are fetters, both arising out of the false idea 'I AM'. The correct position with regard to the question of *Anatta* is not to take hold of any opinions or views, but to try to see things objectively as they are without mental projections, to see that what we call 'I', or 'being', is only a combination of physical and mental aggregates, which are working together interdependently in a flux of momentary change within the law of cause and effect, and that there is nothing permanent, everlasting, unchanging and eternal in the whole of existence.

Here naturally a question arises: If there is no *Ātman* or Self, who gets the results of karma (actions)? No one can answer this question better than the Buddha himself. When this question was raised by a bhikkhu the Buddha said: 'I have taught you, O bhikkhus, to see conditionality everywhere in all things.'[1]

The Buddha's teaching on *Anatta*, No-Soul, or No-Self, should not be considered as negative or annihilistic. Like Nirvāṇa, it is Truth, Reality; and Reality cannot be negative. It is the false belief in a non-existing imaginary self that is negative. The teaching on *Anatta* dispels the darkness of false beliefs, and produces the light of wisdom. It is not negative: as Asanga very aptly says: 'There is the fact of No-selfness' (*nairātmyāstitā*).[2]

[1]M III (PTS), p. 19; S III, p. 103.
[2]Abhisamuc, p. 31.

CHAPTER VII

'MEDITATION' OR MENTAL CULTURE: *BHĀVANĀ*

The Buddha said: 'O bhikkhus, there are two kinds of illness. What are those two? Physical illness and mental illness. There seem to be people who enjoy freedom from physical illness even for a year or two . . . even for a hundred years or more. But, O bhikkhus, rare in this world are those who enjoy freedom from mental illness even for one moment, except those who are free from mental defilements' (i.e., except arahants).[1]

The Buddha's teaching, particularly his way of 'meditation', aims at producing a state of perfect mental health, equilibrium and tranquility. It is unfortunate that hardly any other section of the Buddha's teaching is so much misunderstood as 'meditation', both by Buddhists and non-Buddhists. The moment the word 'meditation' is mentioned, one thinks of an escape from the daily activities of life; assuming a particular posture, like a statue in some cave or cell in a monastery, in some remote place cut off from society; and musing on, or being absorbed in, some kind of mystic or mysterious thought or trance. True Buddhist 'meditation' does not mean this kind of escape at all. The Buddha's teaching on this subject was so wrongly, or so little understood, that in later times the way of 'meditation' deteriorated and degenerated into a kind of ritual or ceremony almost technical in its routine.[2]

Most people are interested in meditation or *yoga* in order to gain some spiritual or mystic powers like the 'third eye', which others do not possess. There was some time ago a Buddhist nun in India who was trying to develop a power to see through her ears,

[1] A (Colombo, 1929), p. 276.

[2] *The Yogāvacara's Manual* (edited by T. W. Rhys Davids, London, 1896), a text on meditation written in Ceylon probably about the 18th century, shows how meditation at the time had degenerated into a ritual of reciting formulas, burning candles, etc.

See also Chapter XII on the Ascetic Ideal, *History of Buddhism in Ceylon* by Walpola Rahula, (Colombo, 1956), pp. 199 ff.

while she was still in the possession of the 'power' of perfect eyesight! This kind of idea is nothing but 'spiritual perversion'. It is always a question of desire, 'thirst' for power.

The word meditation is a very poor substitute for the original term *bhāvanā*, which means 'culture' or 'development', i.e., mental culture or mental development. The Buddhist *bhāvanā*, properly speaking, is mental culture in the full sense of the term. It aims at cleansing the mind of impurities and disturbances, such as lustful desires, hatred, ill-will, indolence, worries and restlessness, sceptical doubts, and cultivating such qualities as concentration, awareness, intelligence, will, energy, the analytical faculty, confidence, joy, tranquility, leading finally to the attainment of highest wisdom which sees the nature of things as they are, and realizes the Ultimate Truth, Nirvāṇa.

There are two forms of meditation. One is the development of mental concentration (*samatha* or *samādhi*), of one-pointedness of mind (*cittekaggatā*, Skt. *cittaikāgratā*), by various methods prescribed in the texts, leading up to the highest mystic states such as 'the Sphere of Nothingness' or 'the Sphere of Neither-Perception-nor-Non-Perception'. All these mystic states, according to the Buddha, are mind-created, mind-produced, conditioned (*saṃkhata*).[1] They have nothing to do with Reality, Truth, Nirvāṇa. This form of meditation existed before the Buddha. Hence it is not purely Buddhist, but it is not excluded from the field of Buddhist meditation. However it is not essential for the realization of Nirvāṇa. The Buddha himself, before his Enlightenment, studied these yogic practices under different teachers and attained to the highest mystic states; but he was not satisfied with them, because they did not give complete liberation, they did not give insight into the Ultimate Reality. He considered these mystic states only as 'happy living in this existence' (*diṭṭhadhammasukhavihāra*), or 'peaceful living' (*santavihāra*), and nothing more.[2]

He therefore discovered the other form of 'meditation' known as *vipassanā* (Skt. *vipaśyanā* or *vidarśanā*), 'Insight' into the nature of things, leading to the complete liberation of mind, to the realization of the Ultimate Truth, Nirvāṇa. This is essentially Buddhist

[1]See above p. 38.

[2]See *Sallekha-sutta* (no. 8), of M.

'meditation', Buddhist mental culture. It is an analytical method based on mindfulness, awareness, vigilance, observation.

It is impossible to do justice to such a vast subject in a few pages. However an attempt is made here to give a very brief and rough idea of the true Buddhist 'meditation', mental culture or mental development, in a practical way.

The most important discourse ever given by the Buddha on mental development ('meditation') is called the *Satipaṭṭhāna-sutta* 'The Setting-up of Mindfulness' (No. 22 of the *Dīgha-nikāya,* or No. 10 of the *Majjhima-nikāya*). This discourse is so highly venerated in tradition that it is regularly recited not only in Buddhist monasteries, but also in Buddhist homes with members of the family sitting round and listening with deep devotion. Very often bhikkhus recite this *sutta* by the bed-side of a dying man to purify his last thoughts.

The ways of 'meditation' given in this discourse are not cut off from life, nor do they avoid life; on the contrary, they are all connected with our life, our daily activities, our sorrows and joys, our words and thoughts, our moral and intellectual occupations.

The discourse is divided into four main sections: the first section deals with our body (*kāya*), the second with our feelings and sensations (*vedanā*), the third with the mind (*citta*), and the fourth with various moral and intellectual subjects (*dhamma*).

It should be clearly borne in mind that whatever the form of 'meditation' may be, the essential thing is mindfulness or awareness (*sati*), attention or observation (*anupassanā*).

One of the most well-known, popular and practical examples of 'meditation' connected with the body is called 'The Mindfulness or Awareness of in-and-out breathing' (*ānāpānasati*). It is for this 'meditation' only that a particular and definite posture is prescribed in the text. For other forms of 'meditation' given in this *sutta*, you may sit, stand, walk, or lie down, as you like. But, for cultivating mindfulness of in-and-out breathing, one should sit, according to the text, 'cross-legged, keeping the body erect and mindfulness alert'. But sitting cross-legged is not practical and easy for people of all countries, particularly for Westerners. Therefore, those who find it difficult to sit cross-legged, may sit on a chair, 'keeping the body erect and mindfulness alert'. It is very necessary for this exercise that the meditator should sit erect, but not stiff; his hands placed comfortably on his lap. Thus seated, you may close your eyes, or you may gaze at the tip of your nose, as it may be convenient to you.

You breathe in and out all day and night, but you are never mindful of it, you never for a second concentrate your mind on it. Now you are going to do just this. Breathe in and out as usual, without any effort or strain. Now, bring your mind to concentrate on your breathing-in and breathing-out; let your mind watch and observe your breathing in and out; let your mind be aware and vigilant of your breathing in and out. When you breathe, you sometimes take deep breaths, sometimes not. This does not matter at all. Breathe normally and naturally. The only thing is that when you take deep breaths you should be aware that they are deep breaths, and so on. In other words, your mind should be so fully concentrated on your breathing that you are aware of its movements and changes. Forget all other things, your surroundings, your environment; do not raise your eyes and look at anything. Try to do this for five or ten minutes.

At the beginning you will find it extremely difficult to bring your mind to concentrate on your breathing. You will be astonished how your mind runs away. It does not stay. You begin to think of various things. You hear sounds outside. Your mind is disturbed and distracted. You may be dismayed and disappointed. But if you continue to practise this exercise twice daily, morning and evening, for about five or ten minutes at a time, you will gradually, by and by, begin to concentrate your mind on your breathing. After a certain period, you will experience just that split second when your mind is fully concentrated on your breathing, when you will not hear even sounds nearby, when no external world exists for you. This slight moment is such a tremendous experience for you, full of joy, happiness and tranquility, that you would like to continue it. But still you cannot. Yet if you go on practising this regularly, you may repeat the experience again and again for longer and longer periods. That is the moment when you lose yourself completely in your mindfulness of breathing. As long as you are conscious of yourself you can never concentrate on anything.

This exercise of mindfulness of breathing, which is one of the simplest and easiest practices, is meant to develop concentration leading up to very high mystic attainments (*dhyāna*). Besides, the power of concentration is essential for any kind of deep understanding, penetration, insight into the nature of things, including the realization of Nirvāṇa.

Apart from all this, this exercise on breathing gives you immediate results. It is good for your physical health, for relaxation, sound sleep, and for efficiency in your daily work. It makes you calm and tranquil. Even at moments when you are nervous or excited, if you practise this for a couple of minutes, you will see for yourself that you become immediately quiet and at peace. You feel as if you have awakened after a good rest.

Another very important, practical, and useful form of 'meditation' (mental development) is to be aware and mindful of whatever you do, physically or verbally, during the daily routine of work in your life, private, public or professional. Whether you walk, stand, sit, lie down, or sleep, whether you stretch or bend your limbs, whether you look around, whether you put on your clothes, whether you talk or keep silence, whether you eat or drink, even whether you answer the calls of nature—in these and other activities, you should be fully aware and mindful of the act you perform at the moment. That is to say, that you should live in the present moment, in the present action. This does not mean that you should not think of the past or the future at all. On the contrary, you think of them in relation to the present moment, the present action, when and where it is relevant.

People do not generally live in their actions, in the present moment. They live in the past or in the future. Though they seem to be doing something now, here, they live somewhere else in their thoughts, in their imaginary problems and worries, usually in the memories of the past or in desires and speculations about the future. Therefore they do not live in, nor do they enjoy, what they do at the moment. So they are unhappy and discontented with the present moment, with the work at hand, and naturally they cannot give themselves fully to what they appear to be doing.

Sometimes you see a man in a restaurant reading while eating—a very common sight. He gives you the impression of being a very busy man, with no time even for eating. You wonder whether he eats or reads. One may say that he does both. In fact, he does neither, he enjoys neither. He is strained, and disturbed in mind, and he does not enjoy what he does at the moment, does not live his life in the present moment, but unconsciously and foolishly tries to escape from life. (This does not mean, however, that one should not talk with a friend while having lunch or dinner.)

You cannot escape life however you may try. As long as you live, whether in a town or in a cave, you have to face it and live it. Real life is the present moment—not the memories of the past which is dead and gone, nor the dreams of the future which is not yet born. One who lives in the present moment lives the real life, and he is happiest.

When asked why his disciples, who lived a simple and quiet life with only one meal a day, were so radiant, the Buddha replied: 'They do not repent the past, nor do they brood over the future. They live in the present. Therefore they are radiant. By brooding over the future and repenting the past, fools dry up like green reeds cut down (in the sun).'[1]

Mindfulness, or awareness, does not mean that you should think and be conscious 'I am doing this' or 'I am doing that'. No. Just the contrary. The moment you think 'I am doing this', you become self-conscious, and then you do not live in the action, but you live in the idea 'I am', and consequently your work too is spoilt. You should forget yourself completely, and lose yourself in what you do. The moment a speaker becomes self-conscious and thinks 'I am addressing an audience', his speech is disturbed and his trend of thought broken. But when he forgets himself in his speech, in his subject, then he is at his best, he speaks well and explains things clearly. All great work—artistic, poetic, intellectual or spiritual—is produced at those moments when its creators are lost completely in their actions, when they forget themselves altogether, and are free from self-consciousness.

This mindfulness or awareness with regard to our activities, taught by the Buddha, is to live in the present moment, to live in the present action. (This is also the Zen way which is based primarily on this teaching.) Here in this form of meditation, you haven't got to perform any particular action in order to develop mindfulness, but you have only to be mindful and aware of whatever you may do. You haven't got to spend one second of

[1]S I (PTS), p. 5.

your precious time on this particular 'meditation': you have only to cultivate mindfulness and awareness always, day and night, with regard to all activities in your usual daily life. These two forms of 'meditation' discussed above are connected with our body.

Then there is a way of practising mental development ('meditation') with regard to all our sensations or feelings, whether happy, unhappy or neutral. Let us take only one example. You experience an unhappy, sorrowful sensation. In this state your mind is cloudy, hazy, not clear, it is depressed. In some cases, you do not even see clearly why you have that unhappy feeling. First of all, you should learn not to be unhappy about your unhappy feeling, not to be worried about your worries. But try to see clearly why there is a sensation or a feeling of unhappiness, or worry, or sorrow. Try to examine how it arises, its cause, how it disappears, its cessation. Try to examine it as if you are observing it from outside, without any subjective reaction, as a scientist observes some object. Here, too, you should not look at it as 'my feeling' or 'my sensation' subjectively, but only look at it as 'a feeling' or 'a sensation' objectively. You should forget again the false idea of 'I'. When you see its nature, how it arises and disappears, your mind grows dispassionate towards that sensation, and becomes detached and free. It is the same with regard to all sensations or feelings.

Now let us discuss the form of 'meditation' with regard to our minds. You should be fully aware of the fact whenever your mind is passionate or detached, whenever it is overpowered by hatred, ill-will, jealousy, or is full of love, compassion, whenever it is deluded or has a clear and right understanding, and so on and so forth. We must admit that very often we are afraid or ashamed to look at our own minds. So we prefer to avoid it. One should be bold and sincere and look at one's own mind as one looks at one's face in a mirror.[1]

Here is no attitude of criticizing or judging, or discriminating between right and wrong, or good and bad. It is simply observing, watching, examining. You are not a judge, but a scientist. When you observe your mind, and see its true nature clearly, you become dispassionate with regard to its emotions, sentiments and states.

[1] M I (PTS), p. 100.

Thus you become detached and free, so that you may see things as they are.

Let us take one example. Say you are really angry, overpowered by anger, ill-will, hatred. It is curious, and paradoxical, that the man who is in anger is not really aware, not mindful that he is angry. The moment he becomes aware and mindful of that state of his mind, the moment he sees his anger, it becomes, as if it were, shy and ashamed, and begins to subside. You should examine its nature, how it arises, how it disappears. Here again it should be remembered that you should not think 'I am angry', or of 'my anger'. You should only be aware and mindful of the state of an angry mind. You are only observing and examining an angry mind objectively. This should be the attitude with regard to all sentiments, emotions, and states of mind.

Then there is a form of 'meditation' on ethical, spiritual and intellectual subjects. All our studies, reading, discussions, conversation and deliberations on such subjects are included in this 'meditation'. To read this book, and to think deeply about the subjects discussed in it, is a form of meditation. We have seen earlier [1] that the conversation between Khemaka and the group of monks was a form of meditation which led to the realization of Nirvāṇa.

So, according to this form of meditation, you may study, think, and deliberate on the Five Hindrances (*Nīvaraṇa*), namely:

1. lustful desires (*kāmacchanda*),
2. ill-will, hatred or anger (*vyāpāda*),
3. torpor and languor (*thīna-middha*),
4. restlessness and worry (*uddhacca-kukkucca*),
5. sceptical doubts (*vicikicchā*).

These five are considered as hindrances to any kind of clear understanding, as a matter of fact, to any kind of progress. When one is over-powered by them and when one does not know how to get rid of them, then one cannot understand right and wrong, or good and bad.

One may also 'meditate' on the Seven Factors of Illumination (*Bojjhaṅga*). They are:

[1] See above p. 65.

1. Mindfulness (*sati*), i.e., to be aware and mindful in all activities and movements both physical and mental, as we discussed above.
2. Investigation and research into the various problems of doctrine (*dhamma-vicaya*). Included here are all our religious, ethical and philosophical studies, reading, researches, discussions, conversation, even attending lectures relating to such doctrinal subjects.
3. Energy (*viriya*), to work with determination till the end.
4. Joy (*pīti*), the quality quite contrary to the pessimistic, gloomy or melancholic attitude of mind.
5. Relaxation (*passaddhi*) of both body and mind. One should not be stiff physically or mentally.
6. Concentration (*samādhi*), as discussed above.
7. Equanimity (*upekkhā*), i.e., to be able to face life in all its vicissitudes with calm of mind, tranquility, without disturbance.

To cultivate these qualities the most essential thing is a genuine wish, will, or inclination. Many other material and spiritual conditions conducive to the development of each quality are described in the texts.

One may also 'meditate' on such subjects as the Five Aggregates investigating the question 'What is a being?' or 'What is it that is called I?', or on the Four Noble Truths, as we discussed above. Study and investigation of those subjects constitute this fourth form of meditation, which leads to the realization of Ultimate Truth.

Apart from those we have discussed here, there are many other subjects of meditation, traditionally forty in number, among which mention should be made particularly of the four Sublime States: (*Brahma-vihāra*): (1) extending unlimited, universal love and good-will (*mettā*) to all living beings without any kind of discrimination, 'just as a mother loves her only child'; (2) compassion (*karuṇā*) for all living beings who are suffering, in trouble and affliction; (3) sympathetic joy (*muditā*) in others' success, welfare and happiness; and (4) equanimity (*upekkhā*) in all vicissitudes of life.

CHAPTER VIII

WHAT THE BUDDHA TAUGHT AND THE WORLD TODAY

There are some who believe that Buddhism is so lofty and sublime a system that it cannot be practised by ordinary men and women in this workaday world of ours, and that one has to retire from it to a monastery, or to some quiet place, if one desires to be a true Buddhist.

This is a sad misconception, due evidently to a lack of understanding of the teaching of the Buddha. People run to such hasty and wrong conclusions as a result of their hearing, or reading casually, something about Buddhism written by someone, who, as he has not understood the subject in all its aspects, gives only a partial and lopsided view of it. The Buddha's teaching is meant not only for monks in monasteries, but also for ordinary men and women living at home with their families. The Noble Eightfold Path, which is the Buddhist way of life, is meant for all, without distinction of any kind.

The vast majority of people in the world cannot turn monk, or retire into caves or forests. However noble and pure Buddhism may be, it would be useless to the masses of mankind if they could not follow it in their daily life in the world of today. But if you understand the spirit of Buddhism correctly (and not only its letter), you can surely follow and practise it while living the life of an ordinary man.

There may be some who find it easier and more convenient to accept Buddhism, if they do live in a remote place, cut off from the society of others. Others may find that that kind of retirement dulls and depresses their whole being both physically and mentally, and that it may not therefore be conducive to the development of their spiritual and intellectual life.

True renunciation does not mean running away physically from the world. Sāriputta, the chief disciple of the Buddha, said that one man might live in a forest devoting himself to ascetic practices, but might be full of impure thoughts and 'defilements'; another might live in a village or a town, practising no ascetic discipline, but his mind might be pure, and free from 'defilements'. Of these two, said Sāriputta, the one who lives a pure life in the village or town is definitely far superior to, and greater than, the one who lives in the forest.[1]

The common belief that to follow the Buddha's teaching one has to retire from life is a misconception. It is really an unconscious defence against practising it. There are numerous references in Buddhist literature to men and women living ordinary, normal family lives who successfully practised what the Buddha taught, and realized Nirvāṇa. Vacchagotta the Wanderer, (whom we met earlier in the chapter on *Anatta*), once asked the Buddha straightforwardly whether there were laymen and women leading the family life, who followed his teaching successfully and attained to high spiritual states. The Buddha categorically stated that there were not one or two, not a hundred or two hundred or five hundred, but many more laymen and women leading the family life who followed his teaching successfully and attained to high spiritual states.[2]

It may be agreeable for certain people to live a retired life in a quiet place away from noise and disturbance. But it is certainly more praiseworthy and courageous to practise Buddhism living among your fellow beings, helping them and being of service to them. It may perhaps be useful in some cases for a man to live in retirement for a time in order to improve his mind and character, as preliminary moral, spiritual and intellectual training, to be strong enough to come out later and help others. But if a man lives all his life in solitude, thinking only of his own happiness and 'salvation', without caring for his fellows, this surely is not in keeping with the Buddha's teaching which is based on love, compassion, and service to others.

One might now ask: If a man can follow Buddhism while living the life of an ordinary layman, why was the Sangha, the Order of monks, established by the Buddha? The Order provides opportunity for those who are willing to devote their lives not

[1]M I (PTS), pp. 30-31.
[2]*Ibid.*, pp. 490 ff.

only to their own spiritual and intellectual development, but also to the service of others. An ordinary layman with a family cannot be expected to devote his whole life to the service of others, whereas a monk, who has no family responsibilities or any other worldly ties, is in a position to devote his whole life 'for the good of the many, for the happiness of the many' according to the Buddha's advice. That is how in the course of history, the Buddhist monastery became not only a spiritual centre, but also a centre of learning and culture.

The *Sigāla-sutta* (No. 31 of the *Dīgha-nikāya*) shows with what great respect the layman's life, his family and social relations are regarded by the Buddha.

A young man named Sigāla used to worship the six cardinal points of the heavens—east, south, west, north, nadir and zenith—in obeying and observing the last advice given him by his dying father. The Buddha told the young man that in the 'noble discipline' (*ariyassa vinaye*) of his teaching the six directions were different. According to his 'noble discipline' the six directions were: east: parents; south: teachers; west: wife and children; north: friends, relatives and neighbours; nadir: servants, workers and employees; zenith: religious men.

'One should worship these six directions' said the Buddha. Here the word 'worship' (*namasseyya*) is very significant, for one worships something sacred, something worthy of honour and respect. These six family and social groups mentioned above are treated in Buddhism as sacred, worthy of respect and worship. But how is one to 'worship' them? The Buddha says that one could 'worship' them only by performing one's duties towards them. These duties are explained in his discourse to Sigāla.

First: Parents are sacred to their children. The Buddha says: 'Parents are called Brahma' (*Brahmāti mātāpitaro*). The term *Brahma* denotes the highest and most sacred conception in Indian thought, and in it the Buddha includes parents. So in good Buddhist families at the present time children literally 'worship' their parents every day, morning and evening. They have to perform certain duties towards their parents according to the 'noble discipline': they should look after their parents in their old age; should do whatever they have to do on their behalf; should maintain the honour of the family and continue the family tradition;

should protect the wealth earned by their parents; and perform their funeral rites after their death. Parents, in their turn, have certain responsibilities towards their children: they should keep their children away from evil courses; should engage them in good and profitable activities; should give them a good education; should marry them into good families; and should hand over the property to them in due course.

Second: The relation between teacher and pupil: a pupil should respect and be obedient to his teacher; should attend to his needs if any; should study earnestly. And the teacher, in his turn, should train and shape his pupil properly; should teach him well; should introduce him to his friends; and should try to procure him security or employment when his education is over.

Third: The relation between husband and wife: love between husband and wife is considered almost religious or sacred. It is called *sadāra-Brahmacariya* 'sacred family life'. Here, too, the significance of the term *Brahma* should be noted: the highest respect is given to this relationship. Wives and husbands should be faithful, respectful and devoted to each other, and they have certain duties towards each other: the husband should always honour his wife and never be wanting in respect to her; he should love her and be faithful to her; should secure her position and comfort; and should please her by presenting her with clothing and jewellery. (The fact that the Buddha did not forget to mention even such a thing as the gifts a husband should make to his wife shows how understanding and sympathetic were his humane feelings towards ordinary human emotions.) The wife, in her turn, should supervise and look after household affairs; should entertain guests, visitors, friends, relatives and employees; should love and be faithful to her husband; should protect his earnings; should be clever and energetic in all activities.

Fourth: The relation between friends, relatives and neighbours: they should be hospitable and charitable to one another; should speak pleasantly and agreeably; should work for each other's welfare; should be on equal terms with one another; should not quarrel among themselves; should help each other in need; and should not forsake each other in difficulty.

Fifth: The relation between master and servant: the master or the employer has several obligations towards his servant or his employee: work should be assigned according to ability and capacity; adequate wages should be paid; medical needs should be provided; occasional donations or bonuses should be granted. The servant or employee, in his turn, should be diligent and not lazy; honest and obedient and not cheat his master; he should be earnest in his work.

Sixth: The relation between the religious (lit. recluses and brāhmaṇas) and the laity: lay people should look after the material needs of the religious with love and respect; the religious with a loving heart should impart knowledge and learning to the laity, and lead them along the good path away from evil.

We see then that the lay life, with its family and social relations, is included in the 'noble discipline', and is within the framework of the Buddhist way of life, as the Buddha envisaged it.

So in the *Saṃyutta-nikāya*, one of the oldest Pali texts, Sakka, the king of the gods (*devas*), declares that he worships not only the monks who live a virtuous holy life, but also 'lay disciples (*upāsaka*) who perform meritorious deeds, who are virtuous, and maintain their families righteously'.[1]

If one desires to become a Buddhist, there is no initiation ceremony (or baptism) which one has to undergo. (But to become a *bhikkhu*, a member of the Order of the *Sangha*, one has to undergo a long process of disciplinary training and education.) If one understands the Buddha's teaching, and if one is convinced that his teaching is the right Path and if one tries to follow it, then one is a Buddhist. But according to the unbroken age-old tradition in Buddhist countries, one is considered a Buddhist if one takes the Buddha, the *Dhamma* (the Teaching) and the *Sangha* (the Order of Monks)—generally called 'the Triple-Gem'—as one's refuges, and undertakes to observe the Five Precepts (*Pañca-sīla*)—the minimum moral obligations of a lay Buddhist—(1) not to destroy life, (2) not to steal, (3) not to commit adultery, (4) not to tell lies, (5) not to take intoxicating drinks—reciting the formulas given in the ancient texts. On religious occasions Buddhists in congregation usually recite these formulas, following the lead of a Buddhist monk.

There are no external rites or ceremonies which a Buddhist has

[1] S I (PTS), p. 234.

XV. The Buddha—from Sarnath, India

XVI. The Buddha—from Borobudur, Java

to perform. Buddhism is a way of life, and what is essential is following the Noble Eightfold Path. Of course there are in all Buddhist countries simple and beautiful ceremonies on religious occasions. There are shrines with statues of the Buddha, *stūpas* or *dāgābas* and Bo-trees in monasteries where Buddhists worship, offer flowers, light lamps and burn incense. This should not be likened to prayer in theistic religions; it is only a way of paying homage to the memory of the Master who showed the way. These traditional observances, though inessential, have their value in satisfying the religious emotions and needs of those who are less advanced intellectually and spiritually, and helping them gradually along the Path.

Those who think that Buddhism is interested only in lofty ideals, high moral and philosophical thought, and that it ignores the social and economic welfare of people, are wrong. The Buddha was interested in the happiness of men. To him happiness was not possible without leading a pure life based on moral and spiritual principles. But he knew that leading such a life was hard in unfavourable material and social conditions.

Buddhism does not consider material welfare as an end in itself: it is only a means to an end—a higher and nobler end. But it is a means which is indispensable, indispensable in achieving a higher purpose for man's happiness. So Buddhism recognizes the need of certain minimum material conditions favourable to spiritual success—even that of a monk engaged in meditation in some solitary place.[1]

The Buddha did not take life out of the context of its social and economic background; he looked at it as a whole, in all its social, economic and political aspects. His teachings on ethical, spiritual and philosophical problems are fairly well known. But little is known, particularly in the West, about his teaching on social, economic and political matters. Yet there are numerous discourses dealing with these scattered throughout the ancient Buddhist texts. Let us take only a few examples.

The *Cakkavattisīhanāda-sutta* of the *Dīgha-nikāya* (No. 26) clearly states that poverty (*dāḷiddiya*) is the cause of immorality and crimes

[1]MA I (PTS), p. 290 f. (Buddhist monks, members of the order of the *Sangha*, are not expected to have personal property, but they are allowed to hold communal (*Sanghika*) property).

such as theft, falsehood, violence, hatred, cruelty, etc. Kings in ancient times, like governments today, tried to suppress crime through punishment. The *Kūṭadanta-sutta* of the same *Nikāya* explains how futile this is. It says that this method can never be successful. Instead the Buddha suggests that, in order to eradicate crime, the economic condition of the people should be improved: grain and other facilities for agriculture should be provided for farmers and cultivators; capital should be provided for traders and those engaged in business; adequate wages should be paid to those who are employed. When people are thus provided for with opportunities for earning a sufficient income, they will be contented, will have no fear or anxiety, and consequently the country will be peaceful and free from crime.[1]

Because of this, the Buddha told lay people how important it is to improve their economic condition. This does not mean that he approved of hoarding wealth with desire and attachment, which is against his fundamental teaching, nor did he approve of each and every way of earning one's livelihood. There are certain trades like the production and sale of armaments, which he condemns as evil means of livelihood, as we saw earlier.[2]

A man named Dīghajānu once visited the Buddha and said: 'Venerable Sir, we are ordinary lay men, leading the family life with wife and children. Would the Blessed One teach us some doctrines which will be conducive to our happiness in this world and hereafter.'

The Buddha tells him that there are four things which are conducive to a man's happiness in this world: First: he should be skilled, efficient, earnest, and energetic in whatever profession he is engaged, and he should know it well (*uṭṭhāna-sampadā*); second: he should protect his income, which he has thus earned righteously, with the sweat of his brow (*ārakkha-sampadā*); (This refers to protecting wealth from thieves, etc. All these ideas should be considered against the background of the period.) third: he should have good friends (*kalyāṇa-mitta*) who are faithful, learned, virtuous, liberal and intelligent, who will help him along the right path away from evil; fourth: he should spend reasonably, in proportion to his income, neither too much nor too little,

[1]D I (Colombo, 1929), p. 101.

[2]See above p. 47.

i.e., he should not hoard wealth avariciously, nor should he be extravagant—in other words he should live within his means (*samajīvikatā*).

Then the Buddha expounds the four virtues conducive to a layman's happiness hereafter: (1) *Saddhā*: he should have faith and confidence in moral, spiritual and intellectual values; (2) *Sīla*: he should abstain from destroying and harming life, from stealing and cheating, from adultery, from falsehood, and from intoxicating drinks; (3) *Cāga*: he should practise charity, generosity, without attachment and craving for his wealth; (4) *Paññā*: he should develop wisdom which leads to the complete destruction of suffering, to the realization of Nirvāṇa.[1]

Sometimes the Buddha even went into details about saving money and spending it, as, for instance, when he told the young man Sigāla that he should spend one fourth of his income on his daily expenses, invest half in his business and put aside one fourth for any emergency.[2]

Once the Buddha told Anāthapiṇḍika, the great banker, one of his most devoted lay disciples who founded for him the celebrated Jetavana monastery at Sāvatthi, that a layman, who leads an ordinary family life, has four kinds of happiness. The first happiness is to enjoy economic security or sufficient wealth acquired by just and righteous means (*atthi-sukha*); the second is spending that wealth liberally on himself, his family, his friends and relatives, and on meritorious deeds (*bhoga-sukha*); the third to be free from debts (*anaṇa-sukha*); the fourth happiness is to live a faultless, and a pure life without committing evil in thought, word or deed (*anavajja-sukha*). It must be noted here that three of these kinds are economic, and that the Buddha finally reminded the banker that economic and material happiness is 'not worth one sixteenth part' of the spiritual happiness arising out of a faultless and good life.[3]

From the few examples given above, one could see that the Buddha considered economic welfare as requisite for human happiness, but that he did not recognize progress as real and true

[1]A (Colombo, 1929), pp. 786 ff.
[2]D III (Colombo, 1929), p. 115.
[3]A (Colombo, 1929), pp. 232-233.

if it was only material, devoid of a spiritual and moral foundation. While encouraging material progress, Buddhism always lays great stress on the development of the moral and spiritual character for a happy, peaceful and contented society.

The Buddha was just as clear on politics, on war and peace. It is too well known to be repeated here that Buddhism advocates and preaches non-violence and peace as its universal message, and does not approve of any kind of violence or destruction of life. According to Buddhism there is nothing that can be called a 'just war'—which is only a false term coined and put into circulation to justify and excuse hatred, cruelty, violence and massacre. Who decides what is just or unjust? The mighty and the victorious are 'just', and the weak and the defeated are 'unjust'. Our war is always 'just', and your war is always 'unjust'. Buddhism does not accept this position.

The Buddha not only taught non-violence and peace, but he even went to the field of battle itself and intervened personally, and prevented war, as in the case of the dispute between the Sākyas and the Koliyas, who were prepared to fight over the question of the waters of the Rohini. And his words once prevented King Ajātasattu from attacking the kingdom of the Vajjis.

In the days of the Buddha, as today, there were rulers who governed their countries unjustly. People were oppressed and exploited, tortured and persecuted, excessive taxes were imposed and cruel punishments were inflicted. The Buddha was deeply moved by these inhumanities. The *Dhammapadaṭṭhakathā* records that he, therefore, directed his attention to the problem of good government. His views should be appreciated against the social, economic and political background of his time. He had shown how a whole country could become corrupt, degenerate and unhappy when the heads of its government, that is the king, the ministers and administrative officers become corrupt and unjust. For a country to be happy it must have a just government. How this form of just government could be realized is explained by the Buddha in his teaching of the 'Ten Duties of the King' (*dasa-rāja-dhamma*), as given in the *Jātaka* text.[1]

Of course the term 'king' (*Rāja*) of old should be replaced today

[1] Jataka I, 260, 399; II, 400; III, 274, 320; V, 119, 378.

by the term 'Government'. 'The Ten Duties of the King', therefore, apply today to all those who constitute the government, such as the head of the state, ministers, political leaders, legislative and administrative officers, etc.

The first of the 'Ten Duties of the King' is liberality, generosity, charity (*dāna*). The ruler should not have craving and attachment to wealth and property, but should give it away for the welfare of the people.

Second: A high moral character (*sīla*). He should never destroy life, cheat, steal and exploit others, commit adultery, utter falsehood, and take intoxicating drinks. That is, he must at least observe the Five Precepts of the layman.

Third: Sacrificing everything for the good of the people (*pariccāga*), he must be prepared to give up all personal comfort, name and fame, and even his life, in the interest of the people.

Fourth: Honesty and integrity (*ajjava*). He must be free from fear or favour in the discharge of his duties, must be sincere in his intentions, and must not deceive the public.

Fifth: Kindness and gentleness (*maddava*). He must possess a genial temperament.

Sixth: Austerity in habits (*tapa*). He must lead a simple life, and should not indulge in a life of luxury. He must have self-control.

Seventh: Freedom from hatred, ill-will, enmity (*akkodha*). He should bear no grudge against anybody.

Eighth: Non-violence (*avihiṃsā*), which means not only that he should harm nobody, but also that he should try to promote peace by avoiding and preventing war, and everything which involves violence and destruction of life.

Ninth: Patience, forbearance, tolerance, understanding (*khanti*). He must be able to bear hardships, difficulties and insults without losing his temper.

Tenth: Non-opposition, non-obstruction (*avirodha*), that is to say that he should not oppose the will of the people, should not obstruct any measures that are conducive to the welfare of the people. In other words he should rule in harmony with his people.[1]

[1] It is interesting to note here that the Five Principles or *Pancha-sīla* in India's foreign policy are in accordance with the Buddhist principles which Asoka, the great Buddhist emperor of India, applied to the administration of his government in the 3rd century B.C. The expression *Pancha-sīla* (Five Precepts or Virtues), is itself a Buddhist term.

If a country is ruled by men endowed with such qualities, it is needless to say that that country must be happy. But this was not a Utopia, for there were kings in the past like Asoka of India who had established kingdoms based on these ideas.

The world today lives in constant fear, suspicion, and tension. Science has produced weapons which are capable of unimaginable destruction. Brandishing these new instruments of death, great powers threaten and challenge one another, boasting shamelessly that one could cause more destruction and misery in the world than the other.

They have gone along this path of madness to such a point that, now, if they take one more step forward in that direction, the result will be nothing but mutual annihilation along with the total destruction of humanity.

Human beings in fear of the situation they have themselves created, want to find a way out, and seek some kind of solution. But there is none except that held out by the Buddha—his message of non-violence and peace, of love and compassion, of tolerance and understanding, of truth and wisdom, of respect and regard for all life, of freedom from selfishness, hatred and violence.

The Buddha says: 'Never by hatred is hatred appeased, but it is appeased by kindness. This is an eternal truth.'[1]

'One should win anger through kindness, wickedness through goodness, selfishness through charity, and falsehood through truthfulness.'[2]

There can be no peace or happiness for man as long as he desires and thirsts after conquering and subjugating his neighbour. As the Buddha says: ' The victor breeds hatred, and the defeated lies down in misery. He who renounces both victory and defeat is happy and peaceful.'[3] The only conquest that brings peace and happiness is self-conquest. 'One may conquer millions in battle, but he who conquers himself, only one, is the greatest of conquerors.'[4]

You will say this is all very beautiful, noble and sublime, but impractical. Is it practical to hate one another? To kill one

[1]Dhp. I 5.
[2]*Ibid.* XVII 3.
[3]*Ibid.* XV 5.
[4]*Ibid.* VIII 4.

another? To live in eternal fear and suspicion like wild animals in a jungle? Is this more practical and comfortable? Was hatred ever appeased by hatred? Was evil ever won over by evil? But there are examples, at least in individual cases, where hatred is appeased by love and kindness, and evil won over by goodness. You will say that this may be true, practicable in individual cases, but that it never works in national and international affairs. People are hypnotized, psychologically puzzled, blinded and deceived by the political and propaganda usage of such terms as 'national', 'international', or 'state'. What is a nation but a vast conglomeration of individuals? A nation or a state does not act, it is the individual who acts. What the individual thinks and does is what the nation or the state thinks and does. What is applicable to the individual is applicable to the nation or the state. If hatred can be appeased by love and kindness on the individual scale, surely it can be realized on the national and international scale too. Even in the case of a single person, to meet hatred with kindness one must have tremendous courage, boldness, faith and confidence in moral force. May it not be even more so with regard to international affairs? If by the expression 'not practical' you mean 'not easy', you are right. Definitely it is not easy. Yet it should be tried. You may say it is risky trying it. Surely it cannot be more risky than trying a nuclear war.

It is a consolation and inspiration to think today that at least there was one great ruler, well known in history, who had the courage, the confidence and the vision to apply this teaching of non-violence, peace and love to the administration of a vast empire, in both internal and external affairs—Asoka, the great Buddhist emperor of India (3rd century B.C.)—'the Beloved of the gods' as he was called.

At first he followed the example of his father (Bindusāra) and grandfather (Chandragupta), and wished to complete the conquest of the Indian peninsula. He invaded and conquered Kalinga, and annexed it. Many hundreds of thousands were killed, wounded, tortured and taken prisoner in this war. But later, when he became a Buddhist, he was completely changed and transformed by the Buddha's teachings. In one of his famous Edicts, inscribed on rock, (Rock Edict XIII, as it is now called), the original of which one may read even today, referring to the conquest of Kalinga, the

Emperor publicly expressed his 'repentance', and said how 'extremely painful' it was for him to think of that carnage. He publicly declared that he would never draw his sword again for any conquest, but that he 'wishes all living beings non-violence, self control, the practice of serenity and mildness. This, of course, is considered the chief conquest by the Beloved of the gods (i.e., Asoka), namely the conquest by piety *(dhamma-vijaya)*.' Not only did he renounce war himself, he expressed his desire that 'my sons and grandsons will not think of a new conquest as worth achieving ... let them think of that conquest only which is the conquest by piety. That is good for this world and the world beyond.'

This is the only example in the history of mankind of a victorious conquerer at the zenith of his power, still possessing the strength to continue his territorial conquests, yet renouncing war and violence and turning to peace and non-violence.

Here is a lesson for the world today. The ruler of an empire publicly turned his back on war and violence and embraced the message of peace and non-violence. There is no historical evidence to show that any neighbouring king took advantage of Asoka's piety to attack him militarily, or that there was any revolt or rebellion within his empire during his lifetime. On the contrary there was peace throughout the land, and even countries outside his empire seem to have accepted his benign leadership.

To talk of maintaining peace through the balance of power, or through the threat of nuclear deterrents, is foolish. The might of armaments can only produce fear, and not peace. It is impossible that there can be genuine and lasting peace through fear. Through fear can come only hatred, ill-will and hostility, suppressed perhaps for the time being only, but ready to erupt and become violent at any moment. True and genuine peace can prevail only in an atmosphere of *mettā*, amity, free from fear, suspicion and danger.

Buddhism aims at creating a society where the ruinous struggle for power is renounced; where calm and peace prevail away from conquest and defeat; where the persecution of the innocent is vehemently denounced; where one who conquers oneself is more respected than those who conquer millions by military and economic warfare; where hatred is conquered by kindness, and evil by goodness; where enmity, jealousy, ill-will and greed do not infect men's minds; where compassion is the driving force of action; where all, including the least of living things, are treated with fairness, consideration and love; where life in peace and harmony, in a world of material contentment, is directed towards the highest and noblest aim, the realization of the Ultimate Truth, Nirvāṇa.

Abbreviations

A: *Aṅguttara-nikāya*, ed. Devamitta Thera (Colombo, 1929) and PTS edition.

Abhisamuc: *Abhidharma-samuccaya* of Asanga, ed. Pradhan (Visvabharati, Santiniketan, 1950).

D: *Dīgha-nikāya*, ed. Ñāṇāvāsa Thera (Colombo, 1929).

DA: *Dīgha-nikāyaṭṭhakathā*, *Sumaṅgalavilāsinī* (Simon Hewavitarne Bequest Series, Colombo).

Dhp: *Dhammapada*, ed. K. Dhammaratana Thera (Colombo, 1926).

DhpA: *Dhammapadaṭṭhakathā* (PTS edition).

Lanka: *The Laṅkāvatāra-sūtra*, ed. Nanjio (Kyoto, 1923).

M: *Majjhima-nikāya* (PTS edition).

MA: *Majjhima-nikāyaṭṭhakathā*, *Papañcasūdanī* (PTS edition).

Madhyakari: *Mādhyamika-Kārikā* of Nāgārjuna, ed. L. de La Vallée Poussin (Bib. Budd. IV).

Mh-Sutralankara: *Mahāyāna-sūtrālaṅkāra* of Asanga, ed. Sylvain Levy (Paris, 1907).

Mhvg: *Mahāvagga* (*of the Vinaya*), ed. Saddhātissa Thera (Alutgama, 1922).

PTS: Pali Text Society of London.

Prmj: *Paramatthajotikā* (PTS edition).

S: *Saṃyutta-nikāya* (PTS edition).

Sarattha: *Sāratthappakāsinī* (PTS edition).

Sn: *Suttanipāta* (PTS edition).

Ud: *Udāna* (Colombo, 1929).

Vibh: *Vibhaṅga* (PTS edition).

Vism: *Visuddhimagga* (PTS edition).

Selected Bibliography

FOR THE ENGLISH READER

ARNOLD, SIR EDWIN: *The Light of Asia* (in many editions).

BURTT, EDWIN A.: *The Teaching of the Compassionate Buddha* (The New American Library, 1955).

CONZE, HORNER, SNELLGROW, WALEY: *Buddhist Texts Through the Ages* (Bruno Cassirer, Oxford).

DALKE, PAUL: *Buddhism* (Macmillan, London); *Buddhist Essays* (Macmillan, London); *Buddhism and Science* (Macmillan, London).

DHAMMAPALA, BHIKKHU: *Basic Buddhism* (The Associated Newspapers of Ceylon, Ltd., Colombo).

EVOLA, J.: *The Doctrine of Awakening* (Luzac & Co., London).

HUMPHREYS, CHRISTMAS: *Buddhism* (Pelican Series).

LOUNSBERY, G. CONSTANT: *Buddhist Meditation* (Luzac & Co., London).

LUDOWYK, E. F. C.: *The Footprint of the Buddha* (George Allen & Unwin, London, 1958).

MALALASEKERA, G. P.: *The Buddha and His Teachings* (The Lanka Bauddha Mandalaya, Colombo).

NARADA, MAHATHERA: *Buddhism in a Nutshell* (The Associated Newspapers of Ceylon, Colombo).

NYANAPONIKA, THERA: *Manual of Buddhism* (The Associated Newspapers of Ceylon, Colombo); *The Heart of Buddhist Meditation* (Colombo, 1954).

NYANATILOKA, MAHATHERA: *The Essence of Buddhism* (The Associated Newspapers of Ceylon, Colombo); *The Fundamentals of Buddhism* (The Associated Newspapers of Ceylon, Colombo); *The Word of the Buddha* (The Associated Newspapers of Ceylon, Colombo).

RAHULA, WALPOLA: *History of Buddhism in Ceylon* (M. D. Gunasena & Co., Colombo, 1956).

RHYS DAVIDS, T. W.: *Buddhism, American Lectures* (Putnam, London).

SURIYABONGS, DR. LUANG: *Buddhism in the Light of Modern Scientific Ideas* (Bangkok, Thailand).

TACHIBANA, S.: *The Ethics of Buddhism* (The Maha Bodhi Society, Colombo).

THOMAS, E. J.: *Early Buddhist Scriptures* (Kegan Paul, London); *The Life of Buddha as Legend and History* (Kegan Paul, London); *History of Buddhist Thought* (Kegan Paul, London); *The Road to Nirvāṇa* (The Wisdom of the East Series, John Murray, London); *The Quest of Enlightenment* (John Murray, London).

WARREN, HENRY CLARK: *Buddhism in Translation* (Harvard University Press, U.S.A.).

WOODWARD, F. L.: *Some Sayings of the Buddha* (World's Classics, Oxford); *The Buddha's Path of Virtue* (The Translation of the *Dhammapada*) (Adyar, Madras, India).

Glossary

Ācariya, teacher.

Ācariya-muṭṭhi, 'closed fist of the teacher', i.e., esoteric doctrine, secret teaching.

Adhamma, evil, wrong, unjust, immoral.

Adhimokkha, determination.

Ādīnava, evil consequence, danger, unsatisfactoriness.

Āhāra, nutriment.

Ajjava, honesty, integrity.

Akkodha, freedom from hatred.

Akusala, unwholesome, demerit, wrong, bad, evil.

Ālaya-vijñāna, 'store-consciousness'.

Amata (Skt. *Amṛta*), immortality, synonym for Nirvāṇa.

Anāgāmi, 'Non-returner', the third stage in the realization of Nirvāṇa.

Ānāpānasati, mindfulness of in-and-out-breathing, a form of meditation.

Anatta, No-Soul, No-Self.

Anicca, impermanent.

Arahant, one who is free from all fetters, defilements and impurities through the realization of Nirvāṇa in the fourth and final stage, and who is free from rebirth.

Ariya-aṭṭhaṅgika-magga, Noble Eightfold Path.

Ariya-sacca, Noble Truth.

Assāda, enjoyment, attraction.

Atakkāvacara, beyond logic.

Ātman (Pali *Attā*), soul, self, ego.

Attadīpa, holding oneself as one's own island (protection).

Attasaraṇa, holding oneself as one's own refuge.

Avihiṃsā (=*Ahiṃsā*), non-violence.

Avijjā, ignorance, illusion, delusion.

Avirodha, non-obstruction, non-opposition.

Āvuso, friend (form of address among equals).

Avyākata (with regard to problems) unexplained, not declared; (ethically) neutral, (neither good nor bad).

Āyasmā, venerable.

Āyatana, 'Sphere'. Six internal spheres: eye, ear, nose, tongue, body and mind; six external speres: visible form, sound, odour, taste, tangible things and mind-objects (ideas, thoughts, conceptions).

Bhaiṣajya-guru, Doctor of Medicine.

Bhante, Sir, Venerable Sir.

Bhava, becoming, existence, continuity.

Bhāvanā, 'meditation', mental culture.

Bhikkhu, Buddhist monk, mendicant monk.

Bhisakka, doctor, physician.

Bodhi, *Bo-tree*, the Tree of Wisdom, *Ficus religiosa*, the tree under which the Buddha attained Enlightenment.

Bojjhaṅga, factors of Enlightenment.

Brahma, supreme being, creator of the universe.

Brāhmaṇa, a Brahmin, member of the highest caste in India.

Brahma-vihāra, supreme dwelling (in universal love, compassion, sympathetic joy and equanimity).

Buddha, Awakened One, Enlightened One.

Cetanā, volition.

Chanda, will.

Citta, mind.

Cittekaggatā, one-pointedness of mind.

Dāgāba, Sinhalese word derived from Pali *Dhātu-gabbha* or Skt. *Dhātu-garbha* which means lit. 'relic-chamber'; a dome-like solid structure in which the relics of the Buddha are enshrined; a *stūpa*.

Dāna, charity.

Dasa-rāja-dhamma, the Ten Duties of the King.

Deva, a deity, a celestial being, a god.

Dhamma (Skt. *Dharma*), Truth, Teaching, doctrine, righteousness, piety, morality, justice, nature, all things and states conditioned or unconditioned, etc.

Dhamma-cakka, wheel of Truth.

Dhamma-cakkhu, 'Eye of Truth'.

Dhamma-vicaya, search of Truth.

Dhamma-vijaya, conquest by piety.

Dhyāna, 'trance', *recueillement*, a state of mind achieved through higher meditation.

Dosa, anger, hatred, ill-will.

Dravya, substance.

Dukkha, suffering, conflict, unsatisfactoriness, unsubstantiality, emptiness.

Ehi-passika, lit. 'Come and see", a phrase used to describe the teaching of the Buddha.

Hīnayāna, 'Small Vehicle', a term coined and used by the Mahāyānists referring to earlier orthodox sects (or schools) of Buddhism. See *Mahāyāna* and *Theravāda.*

Indriya, faculty, a sense-faculty, a sense-organ.

Jāti, bith.
Jarā-maraṇa, old age and death.

Kabaliṅkārāhāra, material food.
Kalyāṇa-mitta, a good friend, who leads you along the right path.
Kāma, sense-pleasures, desire for sense-pleasures.
Kamma (Skt. *Karma*), volitional action, lit. action, deed.
Kamma-phala, Kamma-vipāka, the fruit or result of action.
Karuṇā, compassion.
Khandha, aggregate.
Khanti, patience, forbearance, tolerance.
Kilesa, defilements, impurities, passions.
Kṣatriya, royal caste, the second caste in the Indian caste system, a member of that caste.
Kusala, wholesome, merit, good.

Maddava, gentleness, softness.
Magga, Path, Way.
Mahā-bhūta, great elements. (Four in number: solidity, fluidity, heat and motion).
Mahāyāna, 'Great Vehicle', form of Buddhism of later development, now mainly followed in China, Japan, Korea and Tibet. See *Hīnayāna* and *Theravāda.*
Majjhimā-paṭipadā, Middle Path.
Māna, pride.
Manas, mental organ, mind.
Manasikāra, attention.
Manosañcetanāhāra, mental volition as nutriment.
Mettā, love, universal love, lit. 'friendship'.
Micchā-diṭṭhi, wrong view, wrong opinion.
Moha, ignorance, delusion, illusion.
Muditā, sympathetic joy, joy for others' success, welfare and happiness.

Nairātmya, soullessness, the fact that there is no Self.
Nāma-rūpa, Name and Form, mental and physical energies.
Ñāṇa-dassana, insight, vision through wisdom.
Nirodha, cessation.
Nirvāṇa, Pāli *Nibbāna*, the Buddhist *summum bonum*, Ultimate Reality, Absolute Truth, lit. 'blowing out, extinction'.
Nissaraṇa, freedom, liberation, lit. 'going out'.
Nīvaraṇa, hindrance, obstruction.

Pañcakkhandha, Five Aggregates (matter, sensation, perception. mental activities and consciousness).
Paññā, wisdom.
Paramattha (Skt. *Paramārtha*), Absolute Truth, Ultimate Reality.
Pariccāga, giving up, renouncing.
Parinirvāṇa (Pali *Parinibbāna*), 'fully blowing out', the final passing away of the Buddha or an Arahant.
Passaddhi, relaxation.
Paṭicca-samuppāda, Conditioned Genesis, (Dependent Origination).
Paṭigha, repugnance, anger.
Paṭisotagāmi, going against the current.
Paṭivedha, penetration, deep understanding.
Phassa, contact.
Phassāhāra, contact as nutriment, (contact of internal sense-faculties with the external world as nutriment).
Pīti, joy.
Puggala, Skt. *Pudgala*, individual, person.

Rāga, lust, desire.
Ratanattaya, Triple-Gem: the Buddha, the Dhamma (his Teaching) and the Sangha (the Order of Monks).
Rūpa, matter, form.

Sacca (Skt. *Satya*), Truth.
Saddhā, Skt. *Śraddhā*, confidence (faith, belief).
Sakadāgāmi, 'Once-Returner', the second stage in the realization of Nirvāṇa.
Sakkāya-diṭṭhi, belief in a Soul or Self.
Saḷāyatana, six spheres. See *Āyatana*.

Samādhi, concentration attained through higher meditation; mental discipline.
Samajīvikatā, living within one's means.
Samatha, tranquility, concentration.
Saṃkhāra, saṃkhata, conditioned things and states.
Sammā-ājīva, right livelihood.
Sammā-diṭṭhi, right view.
Sammā-kammanta, right action.
Sammā-samādhi, right concentration.
Sammā-saṃkappa, right thought.
Sammā-sati, right mindfulness.
Sammā-vācā, right speech.
Sammā-vāyāma, right effort.
Sammuti, convention, *sammuti-sacca*, conventional truth.
Saṃsāra, continuity of existence, cycle of existence.
Samudaya, arising, origin of *dukkha*, the Second Noble Truth.
Saṅgha, Community of Buddhist monks.
Saññā, perception.
Sassata-vāda, eternalism, eternalistic theory.
Sati, mindfulness, awareness.
Satipaṭṭhāna, setting-up of mindfulness.
Satthā, teacher, master.
Sīla, virtue, morality.
Sotāpanna, 'Stream-entrant', the first stage in the realization of Nirvāṇa.
Stūpa, see *Dāgäba*.
Śūdra, low caste, the fourth caste in the Indian caste system, a member of this caste.
Sukha, happiness, ease, comfort.
Sutta, discourse, sermon.

Taṇhā (Skt. *Tṛṣṇā*), 'thirst', desire, craving.
Taṇhakkhaya, 'extinction of thirst', synonym for Nirvāṇa.
Tapa, austerity.
Tathāgata, 'One who has found the Truth', synonym for Buddha, a term generally used by the Buddha referring to himself or to other Buddhas. *Tatha* (truth) plus *āgata* (come, arrived).
Thera-vāda, 'The system or School of the Elders', considered to be the orthodox and original form of Buddhism as accepted and followed mainly in Ceylon, Burma, Thailand, Laos and Chittagong. See *Mahāyāna* and *Hīnayāna*.
Thīna-middha, torpor and languor.

Tipiṭaka, Skt. *Tripiṭaka*, Three Books, usually called 'Three Baskets'. The three main canonical divisions of the Buddha's teaching into *Vinaya* (Code of Discipline), *Sutta* (Discourses) and *Abhidhamma* (Higher Doctrine, Philosophy and Psychology).

Tisaraṇa, Three Refuges: The Buddha, the Dhamma (Teaching) and the Sangha (the Community of Monks).

Uccheda-vāda, annihilationism, annihilationist theory.

Uddhacca-kukkucca, restlessness and worry, 'flurry and worry'.

Upādāna, grasping, attachment.

Upādāyarūpa, derivative matter.

Upāsaka, a lay Buddhist.

Upekkhā, equanimity.

Vaiśya, agricultural and trader caste, third caste in the Indian caste system, a member of this caste.

Vedanā, sensation, feeling.

Vibhava, annihilation, *vibhava-taṇhā*, desire for annihilation.

Vicikicchā, doubt.

Viññāṇa, consciousness.

Viññāṇāhāra, consciousness as nutriment.

Vipāka, result, consequence.

Vipariṇāma, change, transformation, alteration.

Vipassanā, insight, analytical insight.

Virāga, detachment, freedom from desire.

Viriya, energy.

Vyāpāda, anger, hatred, ill-will.

Yathā-bhūta, in reality, as things are.

Index

Ācariya-muṭṭhi ('Closed-fist of the teacher'), 2, 61.
Action, Right, 47
Adhamma, 12.
Aggregates, Five, 20 ff., 25, 57, 58, 65; Aggregate of Consciousness, 23; of Matter, 20; of Mental Formations, 22; of Perception, 22; of Sensation, 21.
Āhāra, four, 30.
Ajātasattu, 84.
Akusala, 32.
Alagaddūpama-sutta, 58.
Ālaya-vijñāna, 23 (n.1), 65 (n.1).
Allahabad, 12.
Amata (*Amṛta*), 38.
Amosadhamma (Reality), 39.
Anāgāmi, 8 (n.1).
Ānanda, xi, 60, 61, 62, 63.
Ānāpānasati (Awareness of in-and-out breathing), 48, 69 ff.
Anāthapiṇḍika, 83.
Anatta, 26 (n.2), 52, 53, 55, 56, 57, 63 (n.1), 64, 77; correct position with regard to, 66.
Anubodha, 49.
Anupassanā, 69.
Arahant, 6, 7, 8 and n.1, 32, 39 (n.2), 41, 65, 66.
Araka, 26 (n.1).
Arising and Cessation, the nature of, 42.
Asaṃkhata, 36, 37.
Asaṃkhata-saṃyutta, 36 (n.2).
Asanga, ix, 8, 66.
Asia, 5.
Asoka, 4, 85, 87, 88; his Rock Edict XIII, 87.
Ātman, 33, 39, 42, 51, 55, 56, 57, 58, 59, 61, 62, 63, 64, 65, 66.
Avijjā, 3, 40.
Āvuso, 7 (n.2).
Avyākata, 41.

Being, 20 ff., 25, 26.
Belief, 8, 9.
Beluva, 60.
Benares, xv, 16, 61.
Bhava, 39, 54.
Bhāvanā, 67 ff., meaning of the term, 68.
Bhavanirodha, 37.
Bhikkhu, term explained, 6 (n.2).
Bihar, xv.
Bindusāra, 87.
Bodhi or Bo-tree, xv, 81.
Bojjhaṅga (Factors of Illumination), 28, 74 ff.
Brahman, 51.
Brahma-vihāra, 75.
Buddha, xv and *passim*; as Doctor, 17; 'ever-smiling' (*mihita-pubbaṅgama*), 27; and imaginary speculations, 12 ff.; his message, 86; in painting and sculpture, 27; on politics, war and peace, 84; and questioners, 64.
Buddha-gaya, xv.
Buddhaghosa, 24, 26 and n.3.
Buddhism, aim of, 88; and social and economic welfare, 81; religion or philosophy, 5; realistic, 17.
Buddhist, art and architecture, 27; how to become, 80; ceremonies, 81; temples, 27; training and discipline (three essentials), 46.
Burma, xii, xvi.

Cāga, 83.
Cakkavattisīhanāda-sutta, 81.
Cambodia, xii, xvi.
Cartesian, 26.
Cause, of Arising and Cessation, 31, 42.
Cetanā, 31, *see* also *Volition.*
Ceylon, xii, xvi.
Chandragupta, 87.
Charity, 5, 6.
China, xii, xvi, 27 (n.4).
Chittagong, xii.
Christian, 5, 6.
Cittekaggatā (*Cittaikāgratā*), 68.

Mahāparinibbāna-sutta, 2, 60, 61 (n.1).
Mahāvīra, *see* Nigaṇṭha Nātaputta.
Mahāyāna, xii, xiii, 40, 58, 65 (n.1).
Mahāyāna-sūtrālaṅkāra, 55.
Majjhima-nikāya, 6, 38, 58, 69.
Māluṅkyaputta, 13, 14, 15 and n.2, 64.
Manas (*Mano*), 21 ff., 23 and n.1, 65.
Māyā (Buddha's mother), xv.
Meditation, 67 ff.; on activities, 71 ff.; on ethical, spiritual and intellectual subjects, 74; on mind, 73 ff.; on sensations, 73.
Mental Discipline, *see* Discipline.
Mettā, 75, 88.
Middle Path, 45 ff.
Middle Way (Journal), 55 (n.3), 59 (n.2).
Mind, *see Manas*.
Mindfulness, Right, 47, 48, 49.
Möhn, Miss Marianne, xiii.
Mongolia, xii, xvi.
Mosadhamma (unreality), 39.
Moslem, 5, 6.
Muditā, 75.
Mukti (*Mutti*), 38.
Musīla, 9, 37 (n.5).

Nāgārjuna, 40 (n.2).
Nālandā, 4.
Nepal, xv, xvi.
Neranjarā, xv.
Nibbāna, *see* Nirvāṇa.
Nigaṇṭha Nātaputta, 4 and n.2.
Nirodha, 16, 36, 40; *see* also Nirvāṇa.
Nirvāṇa, *passim*. 12-15, 34-45, 65-68; and language, 35 ff.; synonyms for, 36 (n.2); no annihilation, 37; not negative or positive, 37; as Absolute Truth, 38 ff.; equals Truth, 39; what is after, 40; not a result, 40; and popular inaccurate expressions, 41; not compared to a fire gone out, 42; who realizes, 42; as happiness, 43.
Nutriments, *see Āhāra*.

Pakistan, xii, xvi.
Pañca-sīla (Five Precepts), 80; in India's foreign policy, 85 (n.1).
Paññā, 42, 46, 83.
Parable, of the raft, 11; of the wounded man, 14.
Parinibbuto, 41.
Parinirvāṇa, 41, 60; what happens to the Buddha or an Arahant after, 41.
Path, Noble Eightfold, 45, 46, 47, 76, 81.
Paṭicca-samuppāda, 29, 52, 53, 54.
Paṭisotagāmi, 52.
Paṭivedha, 49.
Pīti, 28, 75.
Pratigha, 28.
Precepts, Five, *see Pañca-sīla*.
Pukkusāti, 7, 38.

Questions, four kinds of, 64.

Rādha, 36, 40.
Radhakrishnan, S., 59 (n.1).
Rāhula (the Buddha's son), xv.
Rahula, Walpola, 67 (n.2).
Raṭṭhapāla, 26, 30.
Reality, 39; Ultimate, 35, 43.
Rebirth, 33.
Relation, between parents and children, 78; teacher and pupil, 79; husband and wife, 79; between friends, 79; master and servant, 79; the religious and the laity, 80.
Relativity, Buddhist theory of, 53.
Rhys Davids, Mrs., 35 (n.4).
Rhys Davids, T. W., 60 (n.2), 67 (n.2).
Rohini, 84.

Saddhā (*Śraddhā*), 8, 9 (n.1), 83.
Sakadāgāmi, 8 (n.1).
Sākya, xv, 84.
Samādhi, 46, 68.
Samatha, 68.
Saṃkhata, 38, 40, 68.
Saṃkhāra, 22 and n.2; term explained, 57 and n.2.
Saṃsāra, 27, 32, 34, 42, 60 (n.3); and Nirvāṇa, 40 and n.2.
Samudaya, 16, 29 ff.
Saṃyutta-nikāya, 36 (n.2), 65, 88.
Sangha, 2, 7, 8, 61, 80; term explained, 2 (n.1); purpose of the, 77 ff.
Sāriputta, 37, 43, 76, 77.
Sarnath, xv, 16.
Sati, 69.
Sāti, 24.
Satipaṭṭhāna, 61 and n.2; *-sutta*, 48, 69.
Sāvatthi, 7, 83.
Saviṭṭha, 9.

Self, 33, 39, 42, 55, 56, 57, 58, 59, 61, 62, 64; the idea of, 26; *see* also Soul, Ego, *Ātman*.
Siddhattha (Siddhārtha), xv.
Sigāla, 78, 83.
Sigāla-sutta, 78 ff.
Sīla, 46, 83.
Siṃsapa, 12.
Sin, 3.
Sotāpanna, 8 (n.1).
Soul, 33, 39, 52, 54, 55, 56, 57, 59; *see* also Self, Ego, *Ātman*.
Soviet Union, xvi.
Speech, Right, 47.
Sphere, of Infinite Space, 38; of Infinite Consciousness, 38; of Nothingness, 39, 68; of Neither-Perception nor Non-Perception, 39, 68.
Stūpa, *see Dāgāba*.
Sublime States, four, *see Brahma-vihāra*.
Suddhodana, xv.
Śūdra, 14.

Taṇhā ('Thirst'), 29, 30, 42; three forms of, 29, 31 and n.5.
Taṇhakkhaya (Extinction of Thirst), 35, 36, 40.
Tathāgata, 1, 3, 7, 13, 14, 56, 61, 62 (n.2); term explained, 1 (n.3).
Tathāgata-garbha, 65 (n.1).
Teaching, similar to a raft, *see* Parable.
Thailand, xii, xvi.
Theragāthā, 28.
Theravāda, xii, xiii, 40, 58.
Therīgāthā, 28.
Thirst, *see Taṇhā*.
Thought, Right, 49.
Three Refuges, *see Tisaraṇa*.
Tibet, xii, xvi.
Tipiṭaka, xi.
Tisaraṇa, 2 (n.2).
Tolerance, 5.
Tree of Wisdom, *see* Bodhi.
Triple-Gem, 2 (n.2), 80.
Truth, 5, 9, 39; Absolute, 35, 38, 39; Absolute Noble, 39; Ultimate, 40, 43; two kinds of, 55; maintaining, 10; not negative, 40; not a result, 40.
Truths, Four Noble, 16 ff., 27 (n.3), 49; within the Five Aggregates, 42; four functions with regard to, 50.

Udāyi, 43.
Understanding, Right, 49.
University of Ceylon Review, 8 (n.4).
Unreality (*mosadhamma*), 39.
Upāli, 4.
Upāsaka, 4, 80.
Upekkhā (*Upekhā*), 38, 75.
Uruvelā, 61.
Uttar Pradesh, xvi.

Vaccha, 41.
Vacchagotta, 62, 63, 64 and n.5, 77.
Vaiśya, 14.
Vajji, 84.
Vibhava, 39.
Vicikicchā, 3, 74.
Vietnam, xvi.
Viññāṇa, 23 ff., 53, 65; *vijñāna*, 23 (n.1).
Vipassanā (*Vipaśyanā*, *Vidarśanā*), 68.
Virāga, 36.
Volition, 31, 42; *see* also *Cetanā*.

Wisdom, 49; *see* also *Paññā*.
Woodward, F. L., 57 (n.1), 63 (n.1).

Yasodharā, xv.
Yoga, 67.
Yogāvacara's Manual, 67 (n.2).

Zen, 72.